GOSHAWK POEMS

Colin Simms — Selected Bibliography

Lives of British Birds, Goose, Norwich, 1970.
Pomes and Other Fruit, Headland, Sheffield. 1972.
Adders and Other Worms, Headland, Sheffield, 1972.
Working Seams, North York Poetry, York, 1972.
Bear Skull, North York Poetry, York, 1972. (Revised edition, 1974).
Pine Marten, Genera, York, 1973
Birches and Other Striplings, Headland, Sheffield. 1973.
Modesty (Swaledale Summer), Headland, Sheffield. 1973.
Horcum and Other Gods, Headland, New Malden, 1974.
Photosopsis for Basil Bunting, Headland, New Malden, 1975. (2nd ed., 1986).
Rushmore Inhabitation, Blue Cloud Quarterly, Marvin, SD, 1976.
No North Western Passage, Writers' Forum, London, 1976.
Flat Earth, Aloes Books, London, 1976.
Parflèche. Galloping Dog Press, Swansea. 1976.
Voices, The Many Press, London, 1977.
Humility, Spanner, London, 1977.
On Osgodby Cliff, Curlew Press, Harrogate. 1977.
Windscale: Four Cantos, Genera Editions, Newcastle-upon-Tyne, 1978.
Pentland, Shadowcat, Weardale, 1978.
Some Company (Tea at 40), Genera Editions, Newcastle-upon-Tyne, 1979-80.
Hunting Bunting, Luksha, New York & San Francisco, 1979.
Ingenuity (Wensleydale Winter), Shadowcat, Weardale, 1979.
Spirits, Shadowcat, Weardale, 1980.
Movement, Pig Press, Durham, 1980.
Time over Tyne: Poems, The Many Press, London, 1980.
A Celebration of the Stones in a Watercourse, Galloping Dog, Newcastle, 1981.
Big Cats, Islamabad, 1988
A Second Book of / Look at Birds, Genera Editions, New York, 1981. (2nd ed. 1989).
Cuddie Cantos, Bellingham, 1986/7 (2nd edition 2000).
Eyes Own Ideas, Pig Press, Durham, 1987.
Luigi Pirandello: Navigator, Shadowcat, Weardale, 1988.
In Afghanistan: Poems 1986-1994, Writers' Forum, London, 1994. (2nd ed. 2001).
Poems to Basil Bunting, Writers' Forum, London, 1994. (2nd ed. 2001).
Shots at Otters, RWC, Reading, 1994.
Goshawk Lives, Form Books, London, 1995.
Bewcastle & Other Poems for Basil Bunting, Vertiz, USA, 1996.
Otters and Martens, Shearsman Books, 2004.
The American Poems, Shearsman Books, 2005.
Gyrfalcon Poems, Shearsman Books, 2007.
Poems from Afghanistan, Shearsman Books, 2013.
Hen Harrier Poems, Shearsman Books, 2015.

Colin Simms

GOSHAWK POEMS

Shearsman Books

First published in the United Kingdom in 2017 by
Shearsman Books
50 Westons Hill Drive
Emersons Green
BRISTOL
BS16 7DF

Shearsman Books Ltd Registered Office
30–31 St. James Place, Mangotsfield, Bristol BS16 9JB
(this address not for correspondence)

www.shearsman.com

ISBN 978-1-84861-525-0

Copyright © Colin Simms, 2017.
The right of Colin Simms to be identified as the author of this work has been asserted by him
in accordance with the Copyrights, Designs and Patents Act of 1988. All rights reserved.

Woodcut of a goshawk on the flyleaf copyright © Colin Simms, 1995.

Postscript, 'Essential Elements in the Calculation' copyright © The Estate of Eric Mottram.

ACKNOWLEDGMENTS

Some of these poems previously appeared in the following magazines *Angel Exhaust, Figs, Fire, First Offence, Headland, Iron, London Review of Books, New American Writing, New Hope, Poetry Review* and *Shadowcat*. Others were collected in *Time Over Tyne* (London: The Many Press, 1980) and in chapbooks published by Genera Editions. Some of the poems were also broadcast on BBC Radio North, Radio KRAB (Seattle), Radio KTCY (North Carolina) and another station in Pine Ridge (South Dakota). Pages 11–39 of this book were previously published as a separate volume, *Goshawk Lives* (London: Form Books, 1995).

The essay by Eric Mottram which serves as a postscript to this volume originally appeared as a Preface to the above-mentioned Form Books edition of *Goshawk Lives* in 1995, and is reprinted here by permission of King's College, London, for the Mottram literary estate.

Contents

Gos low-rowing ride, brushing tip-dew scatter	11
we were talking of the strain after the racing has gone by	11
Liddesdale's Goshawk is ghostly in this dawn mist over the Liddel	12
Gos. 1.10.81	12
Hunters in the Wood	13
as commanding their wave action the gos wove the woodedge's laterals	14
ghost moths go feeling-out the outfield holding	14
Grey light, level grey with reddening bars so wide in the east	15
it was dene country, beneath the farmed old plateau	15
Raucous ringing the mating calls of Goshawk soar	16
Mantling Wind	17
greetings, fellow! yet neither 'hi'	18
'Goshawk, male, in prospecting flight over Sweethope Lough	19
Goshawk, for Janet, my daughter	20
Spring: Arrival	21
Summer	26
Gos in Autumn	30
Winter	33
1st March 1985; Basil's birthday	37
coarse-gorse of the gos' eye	38
Stake-Out	39
This bird, 'West'	40
red squirrel running drystone dyke top cowers	40
gaining height over everyone	41
Gos because	42
We were lucky at marten	43
Writing about what is about; a tautology	43
First flight	44
A mind of her own, like any forest fire	44
Better than by 'The Hunt'	45
gentilis; *'of their own kind'*	45
A shrill Goshawk's, or possibly a Cooper's Hawk's	46

'Eminence grise' wields power behind-the-scenes	46
Tommy and I toddled east from Mickle	47
For the sun came up only in his big eye	47
Followed-up from her stake-out a woodpigeon	48
at the enormous nest, a stinking four foot unmade bed	49
Daws over—the pine-tops caw	49
No more than quiver of a forward digit	50
so in my ruses I followed the fresh trail-bruises	51
gyr versus goshawk	52
Pained wailing of a bairn, heard	53
March storms, "all-seasons'," clear	53
'Fox and Hounds' crack about the gowk (cuckoo)	54
sixty-five of a hundred landings in trees	54
Powering deep sweeping wings do not break them	55
Mistaken for buzzard at the Wall loughs	55
Forest Edge, at Anderons' 1956	56
Trivial, appears prospecting's travail	56
Goshawk hunting under Aurora Borealis, Alaska 1973	57
goshawk that from an apparent indolence	58
'Mountain-goats' seem whitesheep to these slopes	59
Woods quietening for the evening; I'd thought of quitting…	59
'Indigestible' Incident	60
Goshawk lifting a new-born lamb, soil and all	60
A poacher and I watched her repel a crow	61
Bright red cock crossbill this sunlit morning sits	61
Boyhood practising for, on sparrowhawks	62
All-seeing eyes in these high Scots pines	62
"The forest is impenetrable because there's nothing there"	63
A goshawk and a scatter of gulls	63
to a murmur of little stirring goshawk passes	64
to a chorus of wide horizons goshawk soars	64
revisiting boyhood To The Lakes	65
Co-operation in 'nature' so dramatically at sight	65
Mary come, she'd have been at least attentive	66
A great, owl-like in larch branches	66
Brightest of mornings of this airmass deceive	67

He knows the dip in the flight-path, the wave-length	67
Goshawk takes Woodcock off the fell	68
Rainfall on the haughland harder and stronger	69
Goshawk Studies	70
Not cormorant, or goosander, though these might	70
In a spreading air of not being challenged	71
Almost architecturally	72
Midwinter dawning black—not yet a morning	72
stands taller than all else upon the tundra	73
one of those birds which enlarge the largest skies	73
Far louder than he has any right to be	74
lost the hawk in flight, low in this forest ride	74
No 'ifs' or 'buts'?	75
Several times thrusts made at a hoverer	76
(Where herons teetered as on the breeze	77
Watchful as the harriers, kestrels, merlins or crows	78
Tynedale, June 2008	79
Six a.m. and six greylag fly over north westward low	80
Gos and Hare	81
for Richard Hugo	82
a young hawk gillside gesturing weakly	83
we sat at the harpsichord whilst she played Bach	83
Hardly a gentle gentilis but well mannered, even shy, self-effacing	84
Michael and I watched rooted as a grey wave lifts itself…	84
Beat of the heart to the beating wing	85
the Scots' scrum half is sniping-ahead, crushes	85
Laconic	86
Privacy	86
arrival of hawk with hailstorm	87
On the Wall	87
we wait until light strengthens	88
Singing, a head	89
Hidden nests of the successful goshawk	90
Early-season that already specified 'Spring' in Kent	91
Imagine pattern a smooth stretched proddy	92
Recognition before knowing is obvious	92

Fell out of the sky, spaced out along	93
Surely, four hours hunting on to rest	94
Goshawk Kills Kestrel	95
shockingly and as loud as alarms of the heron	96
Oh well is me, my gay goshawk	97
I used to come here to think, I used to come here to pray	98
Scattered little feathers; blast in shale	98
Warming-Up and Great Extinctions together, as everywhere aware	99
Very beautiful barring and vermiculation, brown cast to grey	99
These flatlands, 'fat lands', yet reveal unhealed	100
Above waving spreads of Scots pine broadening at their heads	101
landing, steel on stone on drystone capping, cutting its moss	101
Goshawks will be seen, along with kites and harriers	102
The "twitchers" are here, they've heard a vague rumour	102
(After a Norwegian pine forest, I find)	103
Though gosses' moulting regime is gradual	103
No-one reads the 'old masters', or so to say…	104
Hawk-haunted trees—the "spars" also prefer them—	105
At a first nest of eggs, unable to take one	105
There'd been no night	106
His long elegancies grey-wagtail-shiver	106
Distant overall tent-of-the-nomad Blencathra—	107
Disturbance resisted	108
…rain eased, and the bird shakes shafts and sheaves, to stretch	109
Sonnets from Siciliads in Sicily	110
Dante, the language of the people to supplant Latin	110
Hither and yon he flew hither and yon and again	111
Against likelihood	112
Mistle-thrush some call the storm cock sings	113
Red squirrel hurtles from collision	114
pm, 6 Jan 2016 by the river Irthing	115
beating low and slow, barely holding weigh	116
Spaced-out over this Marcher March sky, yet rather a few	116
Though here and there anemones, foxgloves, bluebells shoot	116
Statistic I	117
Statistic II	117

Should it be so expected, so apparent	117
First emergent from the mirk the dark stark pines	118
Above, only the buds, below dark green seaves	118
his broad wings float in on the morning, low out of the sun	119
Onset in reddening sunset now	119
Take the day, be it never so grey	120
Blind, we scramble in a nervous selfish rage	121
As a 'skipping stone' thrown, skimming her billow wings	121
At Bewcastle Cross, aged about 1440	122
Only for a moment, regretted being there	123
coo, coo … coo, coo … coo, coo	124
Return of the Goshawk	125
Degsastan	126
Plenty of rain every day and every night, it seems	126
For Nick, former forester	127
Goshawk takes new-born lamb	128
Below, a mist of light green bloom glows the thorns	128
As I was singing	129
August is their quietest month	130
Goshawks shot	131
Some too conscious of criticism today to display	131
But an eye-opener. Eight fieldfares at rowan	132
Dipper dithering, bobbing on his chosen stone	132
Goshawk unable to halt the headlong chase	133
Boldest, proudest of the True Hawks race	133
steepling spruces taper to spread their spacing	134
of home	135
there is something in any name deeper than the skin	135
At the nest of gone goshawks	136
Teeming rain, and promising to come again	137
from Rhymes of a Country Naturalist	138
Assembly of hirundines, as to migrate	139
High-Fells April 2011	140
Eric Mottram: 'Essential Elements in the Calculation': The Goshawk Poems of Colin Simms	142

These verses are from goshawk observations since 1955; my first experiences of the bird in the wild overseas—anecdotes of camp life, falconers, birds and probable escaped or released individually, few enough anyway, are considered largely irrelevant in this naturalist's view. Few publications, bar the 1995 *Goshawk Lives* booklet, so well and generously prepared by Harry Gilonis' Form Books, have been used; most of this edition is new. I have used almost entirely only notes made at the time, in now well over 500 notepads, and diaries and letters; memory illumines only a narrow broken trail.

Dates appended are those of original notes and/or earlier versions.

Colin Simms
January, 2017

the goshawk's regime, here in England where it re-established itself
thinly for the first time in generations, in spring, and summer dispersal…
if there are any birds about in winter they are concerned with survival—
hunting without being so conspicuous they'd be vulnerable.

Gos low-rowing ride, brushing tip-dew scatter
leaving-swinging lightest bright-tip laterals
After her, nothing. Dawn, all birdsong before
stilled after her passing.
Sun-behind-blind, at the turn she climbed into it
higher as it warmed her head, higher still more red
gos dressing till the blue was back around her
her gray grew out of grey,
day graduated for her height.
Where there in her way the stray soft black wing threaded
orbiting unconsciously, or it had been too fast for prey
into the sleeping swift her talons thudded
reflexes eclipsed both ellipsings.

for TH (based on an incident remembered, last summer)

* * *

we were talking of the strain after the racing has gone by
in the same palpable silence the gos diddles me again:
tucked-in her style, closing-wing goshawk-hurtle
rockets the blind-side of trees lined, ignoring the ride
yet at the nest-tree with a flourish is feet-first somehow
foot first onto its ledge, never a wobble but ruffled-brow
from the braking, not a feather anywhere else seems disturbed
stillness in the sharpness of the needles we haven't heard, hide
rocked by the wind, but not her; she's over the finishing line
Hartle or Hailwood in concentration, or unconcerned
her acceleration in onto the nest-edge defeating the eye

Oliver's Mount, Scarborough
(from '60s diaries)

* * *

Gos *1.10.81*

        Fellow, the eyes stream on recognition
after the hollerin scream
its stream-sense planing its hollow in   below-plateau
eye yellow and yellowing
        reaming out hate   pile-driver riving
eyass-excited, Cort following
        season accessions reason   below barrens earth opens hard
access of gos and secession from reasonableness   human hesitation on land
excess is aggression,   any essence is all-in-eye   yet the bird watches
not either of us, but movement, as if the rattlesnake's vertical pupil
makes no sense of us, and we do not even know what he sees
or what we see or name as seen. Beneath the surface of a great nerve
only partially warms, like permafrost, even in sight we don't understand
manned in each other's space   none of us in the gos's course.

* * *

Liddesdale's Goshawk is ghostly in this dawn mist over the Liddel
so that you'd see Viking features, the character of the northern race
the features of Linnaeus' Scandinavian bird, but it is ghastly silence
that contributes to such deception as much as our excitement as it does,
and as much as quiet makes the crepuscular Barn Owl whiter still
than it is, if you see it in daylight. Mist destroys distance, fills
space and instils a strangeness or fear so that shapes loom and rear
and seem bigger, and a moving shape and a silent movement chills.
After raindark days, there will be sunlight and warmth this mist says now
though we can't see it yet, already the felltops are standing in the clear
and the land spoken by the bird, soon spreads a new sweat from the brow.

(August 1984)

* * *

Hunters in the Wood

This morning the woodpigeons are not down on the mast
where the snow has not even drifted in scatters under the beeches
some morning fox may have dissuaded, but then and first I hear the gun
a rabbit is swung, underside pure as the snow cups in the bramble and fern
onto the shoulder the grip, at risk only otherwise crows and magpies
no burst of birds ahead of these coming, nothing to say they come, upwind
not even a scolding wren's thought-wedge of panic spinned. They have spurned
questing but relaxed at eye, at foot, deadwinter brackens scarcely disturbed
no more than the wind, against it and sound quartering on quarry, in unison
spare unhasty threading a heading an echelon, only one exposed at a time
at the rabbit-lawns, each his part of the noose moving but waiting-on in motion
Ken and his son, gripped for response, loose in readiness each with his gun
always away from the other and from me, man and boy, father and son brothers
they pass this little house, wall, riding the squall at anchor on it part of it
but parting, they go by my smoke and I poke my nose out afterwards to see
shadow of a hawk in the sun under the beeches, burnt powder and woodsmoke choke its grit
notwithstanding the report of gun disinterested gos sits on in the beech crown above
its pearl, to shift only a shuffle after they have passed and at mettle-some
ruffle of mantling, *that's* why the stoggies hadn't come down to a mast-breakfast—
a few notes of red, beadlets of blood on still leaves, the pestering
robin beginning to shake, those long moments after, its breast.

Low Woodhead, February 1988

* * *

> *Ther was the tyraunt with his fethres donne*
> *And greye, I mean the goshauk, that doth pyne*
> *To briddes for his outrageous ravyne.'*
>
> Chaucer's *Parlement of Fowles*, II. 334-6

as commanding their wave action the gos wove the woodedge's laterals
against the wind and out of the sun upon where the fieldfares sheltered
the dawn had been without calm and they hadn't got up off the roostground
into the northeast wind he came and down its grey ribbon out of the sun
its level yellow-rose split the horizon behind him along the fells level
I had been surprised not to find them down on, if they had not been in the trees.
But the gyr had already shifted them from the trees, for the coup coming now
and I could hear and feel something of their fears even of their panic how
the bird into the flock and flicking my wrist passed me with a long twist
that had given him one of the fieldfares, all silent but heavy as if hoarse
and the bird into the woodline on the hill; how the bird folded itself-in of course
itself the tree lost already itself in the other vague birches rich
in the light greys and blacks of the bird and its fructose lichen.

4 July 1990

* * *

ghost moths go feeling-out the outfield holding
both us lost fielders before we go, grey ashflakes in this light
uncertain censering against cicely and hawthorn moulding bright
from nowhere out of the earth the hawk unfolding
furrow from a soft ploughing grassheads spread from his mowing
manoeuvring talon to maw, stalling-speed chopped at the blockhole
resuming rowing the heavier for the early vole.

Northumberland 1986

* * *

Grey light, level grey with reddening bars so wide in the east
opened place on bigger land the bird's one open eye swivelled
the whole stretch to the hills the sun had already lit up easily
so the place was shortened as the light grew to detail
hills still and nearer, a crisper line and then folds of lines
but the eye of the bird sought short distances, dimensions
only carried the brushing lines she launches on the plantation
nearer the earth, sun width of wingspan realised again
that didn't need to touch the close trees brash, and was gone.

* * *

it was dene country, beneath the farmed old plateau
grooves the land has had to the coast since draining the ice
the bird the same southwest by east to the sea, direction
seeing the whole wooded valley, every thorn tree and thicket
picked up the silhouette/outline as a boy, first letter to Meinertzhagen
a migrant or wanderer (James Fisher's opinion, a falconer's)
overhead on the same land's grain, horizon to horizon

      since before there was a coast

                       and roadsides'

Wood Cranesbill nodding and blowing after the Sweet Cicely,
as Northern as each other
the Southrons come and call them   Cow Parsley
cockily

County Durham, for B.B. 1977/79

* * *

Raucous ringing the mating calls of Goshawk soar
sting air, cling us together under increasingly-beating wing
joyous ear after silence Douglas Sitka after-rapture
hours after, wind gets up amplified raising dead-leaves storm
the bracken not yet up spring lost   rupture
embracing   warm
spring telescoped-closed down to March again, beginning.
"Bitter let all sweetness be, let all these apples be crab!"*
Rhubarb-and-ginger jam well-left on cold stone slab
straight from the pot to get its smell, whitewashed larder
harder than when it set, wonder the warmth of its ferment
ice under bog, frogs' courting stun-warms some tundra
the goshawk picks them off in amplexus, leaves skins to mildew
skin off the jam, same maimed dark stain of the discarded.

No chance of sensory deprivation then for us
forest for its shelter, pingo beneath the concern of the *Accipiter*
there already, steadily closing eye the bird is digesting for us
top of the tree, chuffing a little, bones in the gullet, *gentilis*
the complete craftsmanship we mistake for aristocracy.

Some elegance and pride inevitable, Hall and high table prove
choose to live in the world as it is, no academic groove.

Washburndale, May '79
(Alaska, June '77)

* *what this sun seems to say, in the rime and*
rhythm of the goshawk's mating-calls

* * *

Mantling Wind

Rougher-in   North Sea tightening low is   than an Atlantic blow
its raw sou-wester   new-(moon) noise off Cheviot rumbles a quaking antic
its (the) northeaster rallies trees below this cottage, the *higher* trees are sheltered by hills to the east!
                                          shivering rough his shroud, barbs on edge,
    gos sits
crows don't know to rise and go after him

    the burn above the little house is a river;   it's only enough to bathe meadowpipits usually
   leaves its bed behind not in frustration of its course but in sheer (re)   awakening.
              In the wind as much as the dead twig is   I am
wind bends all,   runs all,   in the chimney as in my lungs as if in my spine and its stones
        a tremolo along a pipe, a vertical cliff pipe;   great hills prepare little landslips about their adits
quake, the old lime kiln collects its draught in reverse and disturbs its little hanging of longeared bats.
Shaking a loose slate skittering down the roof like someone committed on skates
a glissading glissando staccato hitting lake ripples, ruffles at the margin
    fox quiet
his den under me, under the hill's old adit, the deer ride on the wind. The gos is preening
in seas of shifting grass and grey as glass the wind is cleaning.

Low Woodhead, Jan '88

* * *

> *for Cort; whether or not the same experience,*
> *this is under a nest-tree. permafrost*
> *Mackenzie: juv. Goshawk*
> *('73)*

    greetings, fellow!   yet neither 'hi'
                its not 'hello' its admonition
cryin's 'greetin' in the North: the eyes stream recognition
hollerin high scream   its steam seeming creaming the hollow between boles subscenic element in this land
eye   all   eye   yellow   and   yellowing
                                    sense   reaming out whole hate   pile-driver riving   spateriver
state-high   as eyass-excited

       season accessions reason   below the barrens this earth opens-up its hand

                access of gos   is   secession from reasonableness, holistic statement
     human hesitation
                         access is aggression: any
 essence is all in eye   in sight   beneath the surface the mighty lens and the perfect
                            sclerotic then understand
the great nerve   essentially   is demand
and the demand is high
                                    at the back-of-the-neck feel it stand
manned in each other's space   now   and wherever we go
   last night in the tree's arms   underpinned   until the same wind skinned you out that
sharpened my eye, your eye   after the eye   the talon   blue-rooted touches sky and grips hard
only air   opening and closing in conversation and
                                                  your hand
subtends some same tension   digits re-read re-rigid not lame re-stirred   fanned
the land frigid to the bird   rejects it   though the screams were heard, parent-birds murder wean
we come upon the remains   you   me   remember gos-hunting grind
remember we've had good rides   and bind   with this one   resists reside'n hard men's mind.

1.10.81

* * *

'Goshawk, male, in prospecting flight over Sweethope Lough
ellipses high-low, west-cast over Lough, water choppy
and air midge-heavy as the wind collects water and midges up
against the screen of the dense green never thinned or brashed rough
sitkas; many young swallows scatter from under the hawk
but his mate is in attendance at the edge of the trees and takes one
only to drop it again' (verbatim, fieldnote) gosses rarely co-operate in hunting
and this may have been mere play, or more play; Mr. Bunting
nevertheless expresses, excited high voice but just loud enough over the wind
that the birds had come in together, rather low and unseen "my bad eyes skinned"
to see them at all; and look how they go away together, chuffed as hell at their skill

(August 1983)

* * *

Goshawk, for Janet, my daughter

Wild rasps redding   for us   bunching blood
nothing heard
Noting where guns in stubble stood
        so big-bold
          blurred-barred
          bird!
rameur of vermiculate scrolled fine black detail rowed
blue out of sun   soft-ash to the wood
shaking its aftermath
alternate brakes of foliage
raking a span   the planted canes
poising a second repeating   birch bark
                                      aspen-pattern
obscurity showed if we could
talk about seeing the gray goshawk

Sept '77
North Yorkshire

* * *

Spring: Arrival

1.

first green on the trees horizons greensurf thorns prick at the feet just shed
mint neat corm exposed vulva the grass thin herbs not yet up to full fill their form
unable to move blend nor season nor day not yet warm
gos rowing ride brushing tip dew scatter leaving swinging lightest bright tip laterals
after which nothing dawn all birdsong before still after the passing
sun behind blind at the turn gos climbed into it higher as it warmed at her head
higher still more red, gos dressing till the blue was black around gos
gos gray grew out of
hilly woods of Northamptonshire the wind has made similar singing in the taller trees,
the subsong North Yorkshire here that pattern of noise without the pressure of man,
the first-light metal tapestry of songs also thinner here one call of a winter bird not yet left,
the mature solid yet liquid chack of field-fare voice as chestnut and soft gray,
rain coming on with heaviness the trees not yet known for shelter
a disused out-house isolated murk settling equidistant around it a fox passing as if it
wasn't there no scents no threats the gos new straight in through the open side surprised
at the darkness flew out again low to watch
gray plover, a flock as one bird drifting north fat with winter wheat bold to rush goshawk
hastily in to shake on the furthest rafter a hard winter's ledge two bluetits had died on
mummified, feathers aging and fraying as draughts dragged dust dry, puffed out by the drying
tension of thin skin till they had the soft appearance of youth again but duller complacently
turning to the goshawk blown as if in sleep together.

2.

spring by calendar, summer by airmass the day after the thunderstorm as irritable of air
as if the thunder had not yet been but there was dust from the spatter up the bush-skirts
toward the river rain had ridge-and-furrowed sand bare from winter floods so that the squarish ends
of the long primary wing-feathers could brush the driest sand into the feather-vanes and this
was dry enough to each raise a puff of dust onto the skin
the same service where thousands of worms had brought up silt-piles on the levee swan was

being enjoyed by some small brown birds downstream but bold goshawk cousins the sparrow-
hawks dust-bathed in lanes with partridges and sparrows and the pedalling postman
saw them using the grit spread during the ice, as much as the soil-sand blown on by the storms of the early dry spring
the season following this same bird had learned this blown sand was the driest, gave the best scour,
fell out again soonest, its grains rounded from re-use since the winds around the glaciers
had blown it off their rock-waste and river and wind and plough had been re-distributing south through the Vale of York since
the autumn after that once the fire ash of a gorse-and-bracken fire at stubble-burning after harvest
attracted the old gos drifting south and east before a crossing to clean in the northerly fine dry loess
of Germany and it felt the same as that remembered and learned in this place

3.

glacial-melt-water valley little into filled land so that it was forgotten by the farmer
a sinuous scar healed over by the machines except its corn grew darker in the shallow
it brought them up from the south, hirundines black arrows skimming the little clouds of midge
even if they were going east to west, here they turned north and the birds of prey already knew it
where it grades to the river there the spread of the bright green was, and the marsh-marigold yellow
in the willowgarth's annual growth so fresh green it bewildered like its birdsong the willow-warblers
leading up to something on the water cyclical yeasty bubbles showed the first sulphur-yellow wagtails
and up to something the draw led, under the skylarks, sparrowhawks had always been, in this
like so many birds of prey in two sizes.
before they had left the land egg-collecting boys knew that, but their continuity was broken
so that when the sparrowhawks came back after insecticide and persecution they were in three sizes
or even four if you looked closely enough and they didn't allow you to do that
so it was not so bad nor so impossible
the males of the new hawks were near the females of the old hawks in size and looks anyway
near enough for the confusion to be allowed in a country that had eight names for Cow Parsley
they were not long about the entry of the warblers and the martins, the sparrowhawks
the bottom end of the dry hollow a natural funnel for the insects finding shelter
in an unpoisoned place, the top end a shallow space where the wind waited
to take their songs away the new farmers who had taken down hedges, trees, fences to enlarge
make every inch pay as if space could be stretched the wind behaved again as in the days of loess

4.

spring juices burst and clung
rabbit rolling over spurting blood upward
like an exhaust the jugular area opened a red triangle so that it grew on the brown
a flowering of the sandy soil in a revolution or two
and didn't come back upright as in buck-boxing
the goshawk looked back and waited but in the air over and over the twenty-acre nothing moved
so it was spring the badges of chopped side-branches of hedges repeated the sandy clod-tops as if
the wind had spiked them there some sharp in the air others just obscurely bare
the hawk stroked so low below the line of the hedge he seemed to walk stalking but there was nothing there
the stir was all along the irregular ditch downslope of all these great fields as if
all life but the menace in it had slid downhill to the casting worm and the cursing wren
moulding mosses and motionless frog
the morning was cloudy high, visible hills if the cows sat down you could see under the hedgerow trees
for miles, the hedges very low and their gaps aligned at the farm business office as if you passed them
as the goshawk did low and fast at grass and coming corn height for the pleasure of it that air
the land a great long slow hollow between the ridges of the western and the eastern moorlands
a holding back the sprouting corn not much cover for the voles until it was higher, the wings
combing it, as any movement in it the goshawk could tell, the length of the sprout not yet
sufficient for its wavelength to hide the runner, the hesitator, but the waving after the bird was steady
where the trees lined or overhung a ledge and the hedges were trimmed so their laterals were trimmed
the bird could winnow along scarcely appearing against the sky except to watcher just below
the birds exploded upward ahead of it into the hearts of trees and bushes once the disused
railway embankment set shrubs gorse bramble brier studded ragwort grassclumps
as convenient as a stream route between the goshawk woods but still open to the goshawk's world
the corners drawn in more than we saw, cloud towers more vertical beyond the limits of our eyes
the great vision where crows merely partitioned   lapwings shifted subtly and skylarks suggested

5.

at one place   beside a wood   where there was good cover approaching both sides of a road
the goshawk could flick across in a second once right wingtip beyond left wingtip
concentrating ahead for the concert crossing-to-be-clear suddenly flashed

a silver cylinder suddenly-foreshortened to less than his own length. In friend fog.
It was a rare thing to find in an English countryside, the thing that threw him passing
an American mail-delivery-box the glint of distant silos hunters may be wiseacres
the same burnish on the uptilt barrels of the pheasant-shooters, though a colder colour
fixed and meaningless here, nailed to a tree-trunk like a trap. It was a trap for him.
Another day and the goshawk looked more closely at it from a higher perch and was seen.
The man whose car and wood it was had the one for privacy, the other for pleasure.
This pleasure was to be in the rearing of pheasants and the shooting of them in season
and no Cooper's Hawk would interfere with that if he could help it. He hadn't settled
in the Old Country to suffer the natural variable he hadn't understood back in the New.

6.

Distant twittercreak of wind marching down unrelated and rubbing trees together in it
the wood nearest the roost alive with such noises playing tricks going and coming
         in entirely different grunting deeper whining periodic almost regular the gos
almost colliding with a great brown bobbing bullet of a bird intent on flick and glide
----------- uu -------------- uu --------------- uu ------------ uu ----------- uu -----------uu
the boundaries of territory going and coming the square plantations of fifty years
ago scattered across the farmland for foxes, pheasants, once for timber, linked
the boundaries of territory the straight stretches of the bevelled forestry roads were
sighting along gun barrels of undulating fetches firebreaking slashing shocks forest rides
roding riding the hawk fascinated followed this lone late unmated woodcock,
despite the fashing of wood pigeons in the woods' gloom

7.

the rain again came on bringing on calls like it was dawn all over the false-spring was real
it was out ideas we heal, the pool the freshet left over towards the Syndicate hut
collared-dove colouring the arid of the over-drained fields the lapwings flicker
little drops the incoming ring-ousel that flacked the tail up hard every time 'chacked'
as if the bird needed to or it was corollary to harsh effort the woods straggled as ground broke
like the lumpy sea poking up inlets and you realise you are wet and the gos did
and found the dry wood corner slowly hanging the long wing at an unexpected angle

but to dry the first moment of real relaxing in this open northern environment
and the one the man out early with his gun and nothing to show for hours
saw the flag blow and the bird turned from him.   Sparrowhawks were fair game,
hadn't they been just about the only birds not on the official protected list
and surely with reason. That law rescinded and the sparrowhawk returned to protection
a recent thing. But not from this line of reasoning that goshawk was shot,
more from what hesitation in the rain can do to exposed expensive special metal.

Summer

1.

Goshawk watched from the corner oak of the wood that long before the planting
had been a hedgerow tree, broad and long-branched, the top dead and gray
so near its trunk where the breeze cooled the bird now the gos was inconspicuous
to the men hoeing with their jackets on in the sun, working most with the breeze in front
only one younger one had had his coat off, you could get bad sunburn a day like this.
Sweat in the eyes all the time, only the eldest bareheaded; the others' headbands
greasy and running dirt over their temples and foreheads. The shadow and a bit to each side
of it each man's strip to work, the eldest man just a little ahead of the loose echelon.
Leaning against the fence they faced a light shot-gun and an empty haversack past bait-
time and the gos shuffled a little to watch the field on the other quarter, empty of men
but rabbit prospects later. A lapwing had noticed the gun and towered, coming down lightly
a field beyond where the distant hill line was appearing as the air cleared toward evening.
Time waiting around was not time waiting or watching: the bird of prey, being, enough.

2.

Waiting around the backing weather coming on light norwester to darken the evening sooner
but still clearly, the rabbits out of their burrows now in the wood edge—once earth-banked hedge
under and along from the gos tree where sitting as if always there the bird shifted only eyes
over twenty yards of bare strip between the burrows and the crop.
Two long oak leaves only rocked, two second-primaries practically touched earth on the drop
and the rabbit pausing at scatter of old droppings was rowed along in an unhurried flurry.

3.

The crowing cock pheasant completed the cloud cover over us, no bats to zag it open
the dawn no longer stood up a wall of sound but it was a day when young birds burst
tail-less, busily but clumsy, buds out of bushes, not ruddered properly and too fluttery
the old gos knowing about them how soft their meat after the cuckoo had gone away
leaving over-stuffed caricatures calling all over the land always a bird on its perch when you knew them

or near it on another the cuckoos leaving the fly as the young gosses had to eyes cocked but oh
so three-syllably slowly it was picking easy one after the other repeating the   presence
                                                                                    finned
tides rocked the structure of their corpses bullfinches chaffinches greenfinches blackbird
                                                                             second brood
staggering the waving   long-headed but delicate *Hordeum secalinum* Meadow-Barley.
only such complicated shapes complicatedly crookedly crisp as the oaks could crush such as
       curled-leaves rattle or slip or sing if they are lifted lively enough but dense-cooling this oak
processing the wind not just predictably waving it as the smooth leaved do, though each of those are different
and these   oaks speak a different dialect than they do in the south the hawk had learned
their   irregular outlines their raised and buckled inlines, their patches of growths, the smooth
raised areas, the hollows with their inhabitants, the galls with theirs of a world of larvae
clinging, eating, dropping on their threads so that the tree's never quiet even on the deadest calm
the birds reliance on this store to feed their summer young the gos had learned and counter-weight
on the end of the limb to be served of all the passers-by to the emporium, just as hunched
and apparently asleep as the almost hovering unreal shape against the beams through the
threadbare parts of the building cloaked against recognition but in its place the goshawk
seemed always in tension, a state of being-about-to-do, the feathers solid as if glass or mineral
or bark they flashed only on opening in the bird's own dark the spark leapt and the bird killed.

4.

Rasps redding for us   bunching bruised blood   except such rasping   nothing heard
noting where   guns   ready in stubble   stood   bullets for birds   barred
before   the eyes   some film   so big-bold   blurred-barred   bird
rameur vermiculate-scrolled fine filtered black   detail
blue out of sun   soft-ash to the wood   shaking its aftermath
                                                  alternate brake of foliage
            obscurity showed if we   could see
raking aspan   the planted canes   poising a second   pausing birch bark
parsing the thump in the heart   for us   aspen-pattern

5.

awkward ciphers wrapped like   Arabs   tree the trial-flight was-to   fledglings
gray   dead   ashraggy   as if balancing its   unequal arms to a cross
so many crosses deal   as we   criss-cross   the hedge   you settle field's edge
we blind have the advantage   see you better   field in belly pit
feel the field of force   sweep the cere fields mustard   wash stalk edge
lap yellow-cered young   their presence constant flicker wind off sedge   there
here not of these iron-aged fields   gentile not celts   but axes
haggard letters young fetters to the   electors of Saxony two untort daughters
beginning to fill with sand   feeling it flow that quartz inside   or hawk
accuses any stance   loitering a curse   bigger than parents   stilted huddle
all wing   all leg   all neck fingering slow on one key   lingering to prime

6.

sought protected   elected waiting to be got or shot   before their time   meant
only to some extent   following the actions of the parent
you learn to hunt by first learning to see: the young gosses walking about on the woodland floor
not unfit to fly, not picking grit, but the corollary of the soar.
The beetles and grubs, even slugs and worms, in the coordination of eye and brain and talon and beak
leatherjackets of the soil and of the air as the voles
and the rabbits   and as noisy and conspicuous in their way to say to the learning bird of prey,   to speak.
on the way to that moment of the first snatch off a branch
the corpse of a rook on the road whose overnight warmth had drawn the grass-seed and kept the corpse warm
both young gosses partook of it, requiring the dismantling of both
the last time they would cooperate like this or with another of their kind until the nest-stead in the storm
razors gripped across the soft yield and locked into the hard spine
the rook rocking the head, their heads, scattered morning forkin-robin pincers up in alarm
the strengthening grip up the vertebrae   grip as the load comes off them on to those ahead

7.

a week later exactly and the gauntlet thrown, the mailed fist hit the scampering rabbit to stun it
and the long rear talon did not bite. At the end of the run the gos rose steeply over a sworn scraped-together call
from two peewits. In the disused barn a mile away the beetle laboured over a long dried pellet and we
rest in presence this faucon gentile the ignorant's coat of arms   pretence lanced
with the Platonic world losing thrall
                                                                                              particularly petulance
stretching the old tarcloth someone had used to patch part of the roof
                        tree   jousting
      reason's nothing to the swing   one leg dangling a jess fling
the midges are not bothering in this bothy   and your breath is as warm, gos.

* * *

Gos in Autumn

1.

The first movement drawn   lumpy stillness   wooded dale long down-grade
song led development, dawn   singled   no matter how often heard
bird brightening after rain a Central-European something   the tableland cut by Sneverdale
horn difficult accompaniment   for strings   Mahler's first warblers trigger
                                chain accelerandi gos poised own calm centre

2.

In the wood still nothing   its own tiled-covert feathers faithful,   bird-song as if held under wing
supporting blackbird's long crescendo liquidly the flow horizontal, pumping mists mouthing east missing space
gos was form and markings   shuffled contours to new pack   on the air light is raised on the song
louder   cloud line changing outline in hill line some same clouds warn worn to warm only long
    relatively more solid in the dawn   to alight a long swell out of forest, coneys red part of the glowing
tilth texture earth for upperbreast feathers had been as light woods to these block forests. Edges, for growing.

3.

Crossgraining Crosscliffe, Raincliffe leaf and light light leaf light light green light   green
the flight merged wood comprehension, images eye brain pine brash spruces flash pattern
suddenly thinning the bird up in response too fast to feel the sun but in the eye its swivel against
air pressure the muscles around it so the head hardly turned the map of the whole moor
southward from the hard centre whistle downgrade toward Pickering wind and blade outward edge
eye stretch wind flickering the wet tipped off the fields in slices a flatbed driven irregular pages
tipped-in moors were history the massive spangles of golden-plover souled in two great patches
mist across rich edges music moving the beginnings of taken ideas and moods dancing on air
reflecting pools the edges of rainflood and the long thicket-lines they put pheasants down at
to shoot them up at and the pigeons the forest gos picked easiest at grey light level grey reddening
slot bars wide opening   grate east place big land birdseye all of it to the hills the place shortening to detail
with light grey, going under pinned nearer crisper line then folds of lines the forest its own width of wingspan
taiga bird, underpresent in American broad leaved forest where the Cooper's Hawk, less able, is more available

4.

Gos sort short distance carried brushing lines with her launched from the plantation to pattern the country
Near the earth, for comprehension you'd climb high but for rushing through poles and brashing precision
           shortened
Rain shaken rare leaf drops never stare: with stars in stormy skies the eyes of spies   surprise
the hawk not the only survivor, gos says I am all beak to you, you classify me by its screw
cruel cutting-edge, you identify me by it, you characterise me by it, caricature the undesirable who
never mind true to calling; clean better than you who are of it as I am not of it, romantically you
justify your belligerence to one another, of greed, of grossness, by pointing at me mere nature red in tooth
and claw: the bird-of-prey is looking all-ways, can mankind see so far as to learn to eat carefully
: nowadays the bird of prey, like the Red Indian, is looking-away: when I am merely the killer we all come to.
Times lay aside this place, this page: you only can come to me if love goes on a-head and first
in the hills the looking-ahead a sonority, seniority, on the flats a looking-away an honouring.

5.

Late autumn rare growth anvil clouds on unstable air but no thunder there, the gos to pleasure feed on air
flying eating it at speed gross, on the north-east drive of the air the gos half closes the eye
half the time the way Freddie Dixon rode, not seeing less but more of what is wanted, concentration
horizontalling wind broken sky blueing then black night to be blacker, new stress the first morning
frost would represent, present, enter the bird waiting on other birds as servant to their species
since the days of wind that brought the autumn in on summer with the spiralling of ashkeys, ashkeys.
yellow light that once in a while sunsets this side or that when the light is level to the yellow eye
shadows lengthen drain into the sun of the gos hardly more gold or bigger than his eye
in seeing them fringed, darker, nearer as if nearer, blinding, stopping to look
away, rest the eye, using one eye, shading one or both, squinting
there's vision in a partial closing of the eyes.

6.

The powerful bird of prey, the good European god representing the fierce European foreigner, not fair
not speaking the language, not aware of situations, begin to assert themselves breeding again in England
in the eyes of those that see them, as if advice from a gypsy, a migrant as osprey or kite or eagle

the sun silver through its high mother-of-pearl cloud and goosedown fog coming on the land
the moor seeming to stretch forever in its linking wisps over the low country threading the streams
but for a second or two the light beat like a quick light pattern of wingbeats of the gos-glide
as if the silver sun blinked at fly-in-the-eye, and there the gos flew in the sun and wind eye
to either side about the glade. The rain was coming, but the sun in the rain was still warm.
Darkbright by airgun terrorist moon trespass boys stumble stark night stubble all else iced
save their clay that does not crumble breasting the rise that lines the little river curves
crest less than less-cultivatable mess, vein farmer's nerves, south still of the real rounded
ridgeforms of the moraine stand-out soft too-modest for levees too unreliable it seems
across the plain the Cau'd beck is an englacial stream like consciousness of evilly directed
its jumble turves slain steam gleam rain wave grass timber first in living then in
retreating ice-sheet, meeting its melting its melting-across the grain the gos spread slain
stain on the mud, colour and no blood. Dying in the cold, forced into containing restraints
the Uis-ge another awkward North Yorkshire daughter 'water-of-life' in the Celtic it was before
warming-stream like whisky the boys pinched intoxicating fingers of, even before they knew them
enter water, under the clod and of the land as the feathers as much of the air above.

7.

The wood stood on its knoll and wholly occupied it, setting it apart, unlikely Pennine
it was the only knoll you saw around and the wood had an even curved top so you could
imagine ground under was smooth and faithfully shown by the trees. The few trees in the lessening
hedge losing leaves were on little smokes but the mood was solid, black even when you were near.
World white that morning, even ditches white in stripes of powderice and ice on old leaves
sun pointed-up differences, not penetrating, waiting for winter. The wood was not penetrated
that, his west side of it because of last night cold east wind. The gos shuffled his hunch, bunched
face feathers, over the new forest filling the valley to the south eye cowled more like owl he flew.
When the wind stopped there were so far few leaves on the trees that evening than that
morning that the gos was for a second uncertain

their green stippling to yellow to bronzes microscopically faster at one end of the wood than the other;
these mottle delicates of Norway mapleleaves, the thin copper-bronze of their keys.

* * *

Winter

1.

Range of turned-slices visible short, the tractor echeloned and leaned a bit, the man inside
steaming-up a little inside, condensation running on the glass inside, gray brown smears outside
hours hearing the motor his father had more likely seen it than he on the old open Fordson
light and black to lichen, lighten it a bit no more. No leaves for the bird to fold itself behind, his
father's eyes full of the sky not so blue but the war brought all this that on the fact of the act
its greatest labour the news spread the whole countryside a leadened newspaper folded and rucked
and the spark not strong enough in the weak light, thin sunlight if it is there at all to jump the gap.

2.

Like the crest of cuesta this Northumberland horizon the bird able to judge to the point in the stroke
where the squirrel stride rise would be flying aligned like the practised cross-country runner knows
adjusting strides ahead to place the protuberant raised lace tree-roots without a hesitation
or the throttle hand caressing the road ahead, that much aware of living in the pace
the little bend ahead and the line for that and that tree slight-turn the one chosen clawscrabbling
the only indecision in precision where the claws had marked sets of short scores across its rough bark
tiles so they came together squirrel and talon without the squirrel knowing anything more about it
than the wrap around through the thorax at the point where the kukris touched wetting flankfur
and the air-fanned tail suddenly loose at the same laws of the dead leaves empty windy hedge.

3.

Deadwater the land uniformly blanketed up hill and down no contours show except the little lines of becks
preserved unreal even this mist frost morning you could be sure they were real though a few beats
disappeared the ride around blend to a spot scurrying ahead calmly like water-boatmen ripples
because of the density of the mist the trees made of hill fog clung to before it could lift
airdew   the sun that dawn drew a scarf coiled planted hills between seven hundred and a thousand feet
dissolving upward in tattered inverted tassels openwork weft rides stitched the place between contours
never leaving its gray-as-goshawk embrace at the top edge waiting to disperse with it roe deer
wisp into hill as its bracken, graying from red and a loose knot of grey-brown old wild goats

the long points of their fleece down draggle heavy with it the feathers darkened a little with it brushing
spittle grass such a small stretch of the dead straight Deadwater ride insight at once, no place
for confidence unless you knew it was, learned to come upon. A red-backed vole disturbing tussock
Aira praecox at last after five miles of it the hunting easier than it seemed, even.

4.

On the dead air it was effort to rise on slow wings what the herons must feel fatiguing
longer and longer nights between fewer pools and more regulated waterways as laid barracks.
Gos had played with one in the air on their way from the railway to the old grainland at height
the massed starlings of winter further north didn't aspire to mob at, and the heron had played back.
Pigeons' conspicuous convergence flung together over the grey-plover stand until they rose and fell
quiet as a shadow across the retina. We are secret people, huddle, come and go as the place does know.
Turning to use the sun to pick out the groundbirds by their shadows the gos levelled to fly alongside one
back-marker, twisting with it and gaining then slowing to stalling speed with the plover alone now
and taken with one foot at the edge of reach like off a low ledge, a flurry of wings to the ground
and one wing shaken out over the corpse like a shield from the carpal joint fanwise forward.
Bringing to mind how the bird had judged to the point in the stroke of the wingbeat a calm dense foggy
morning air precisely where the reach of the mailed foot would be at that tree's protuberant raised-root gnarls
were scored by the squirrelscrabbling its indecision the roughbark tiles so often traversed there they
carried hair of squirrel, fox scent, a tarry of dead leaves the brush of the gos' wing scraping just once.

5.

They called it Deadwater but its streams after the rain and the rivers below made a pattern
of light-reflection different for the riffles when the freshet's running and the currents more
than when the wind is more and its against melt and way and shone and brilliant
at its tips the shallow field in view is silverer than white and there's change coming broad
and definite as night. South running the river seemed to be turning back upon itself light.
The kestrel on the spruce top instead of the effort of hovering worked the close circle, shuffling.
In short-diving jets of white cold air to eyes balanced the pressure of the wide sclerotic ring of bone
and the eyes stayed open so that the individual tops of the black blanket of the square plantation
of uniform pines protruded, carving fresh patterns like fingers run over high stiff carpet pile
and the pattern of ridge-and-furrow of the drained meadowland flashed stereoscopically in and out

of the true peripheries of sight regardless of fences, little upstart lines the gos even learned then, gaining comprehension final for that place; a map where the wet corner rushes harboured rabbits.

6.

The field had a combed-out look after the wind, and the light was different—as if it was permanently a different time of day, never dawn. Shadows reasserted themselves. The birds, even those who had been with the kestrel unable to feed in the wind, were nervous about the first hours. In the light-gathering eye of the gos the crow was black, and the rook was a different colour, though they look alike to us. The streams were not the same blue, the fields were every one different in texture and colour even empty this winter. But the sitka spruces of the great forest, the biggest man-made forest of Europe, were alike. The bird beat between these trees with nothing passing under him, spiky excrescence on cuesta or dull hollow alike. These woods are good for the goshawk only in losing a big bird quickly, or to change pace and direction. The old forests of the border, birch and alder and thin oak and hazel, would have stretched and not confined. The gos had to lift out to fly freely; the planted trees too close for any other feeling than restraint. Not a bird of the sky the wingbeats approximated to the fat pigeons the man was waiting for and he let both barrels go in just the way he would for a really big stoggie just out of range and nothing else had offered for hours. The bird, winged, hit to dull eye, went on for miles to a place it knew the old birches near the stream had the venerable feel such border birches show, gray above and below.

7.

Eye in mine in the presence of the bird quiet and still, the hunch near the thinning bole
tho it is slug-gray as old *Limax agrestis* sliming over those grey stones it radially glows
that bird because of the eye in it and I am in it, in view with no distance, no going away
as the day has been long for both and is now folded and strong: from the distance the sun had raised
a steel glaze on the stubble's three-inch rough cut blaze and the haze of the faraway lost gaze
so you could not have seen the bird still there. The gorse has blooms all the year but their burn
was only as big as the eye, whose fires seem all out but for the glow that casts no more sheen
than the dew below and we were waiting bird and man for the gray wind to come off the border,
to change for the night and its noises to come into range in order. This wood is any wood; old
its trees then were carefully coppiced for useful poles and the thin trees could just hide slight
sparrowhawks—the goshawk's lesser relative. Looking at it, it has to be the individual character
of a bird that confers nobility; a captive bird, its world released from reason, reflex and reaction,

behaves complicatedly towards what it could be, towards one of the changing personalities it could have struck. True feeling in a world removed from sentiment. Looking for its pattern isn't trees carefully cropped: to look me away the bird was folded back into its tree the tree into its branches the branches into their lichen and the lichen into the overcast of the day all gray, not looked-into. Slack.

* * *

1st March 1985; Basil's birthday

Very cold east wind into the house, very heavy cloud with light sleet then snow behind it; the snow settling by late afternoon, and cold. As I'd been gardening, two goshawks had 'prospected' the south side of the great wood, drifting on toward High Woodhead at treetop level and a little below, ignoring the woodpigeons feeding in the open beside the bottom corner of the wood below me as I worked on the open bevel of the kame ridge and picked up a relic of the stone age hunters who had lived or paused here. The gosses were causing no commotion, surprisingly.

The restlessness about them struck me, and it was obvious before they'd seen me, coming blind as they did over Richardson's wood low. and they made no effort to avoid me. I was bent to the earth, perhaps, but able to watch their progress, the male rising above the female in her path, both dithering to the side half-heartedly as if in a weary courting routine without its first careless rapture. He led to the great pines near the heart of the higher part of the wood, semi-circled one of them with an old crows' nest just visible in its highest branches, and settled for a few seconds almost on it. Alighting a foot or two lower, she was off again as he mantled and they passed out of sight among the treetops further with just a curse from a jay and an explosion of a blackbird further off.

In twenty minutes they had returned, and I supposed them the pair roosting most of this winter on the bottom strip of old pine, birch and sitka and open enough to allow views right across the North Tyne from the northern rimrock of the Caller Hues crags to the top of Dunterley Hill above me on the south. I hadn't really changed rhythm, digging, and the light was going in the light snow and overcast, about five fifteen and the fire wanting attention inside. But the goshawks had returned as quickly as crows can, and more purposefully than they had passed earlier; the male with a tiny spray of ivy in his bill. Circling a little, less than two revolutions, around the peaks of the old sitkas (with the form of 'Caledonian' pines) in Richardson's, they pitched it in a rather lesser tree above the spring near the wood's heart, and only some forty yards from me, behind a screen of thin birches and the scrub oak of the region. I was reminded of the pair which had circled over the wood, low over the bottom strip, each October before setting to roost there the winter. Keeping the gos pair in frequent view, but using the cover of the trees down to the bottom strip only a few hundreds of yards away, I searched the high pines there the goshawks used to roost, as they now should be into roost off their hunting grounds a few miles away. Sure enough, there was a male sheltered in ivy from which he had shaken the snow—no doubt in his shifting to settle. And a female, a young female in her first winter, a few trees away close to the trunk as an owl would be. The wind was beginning to rise, and a great purple-blackness in the north lost the Caller Hues crags and began to lose the redpoll wood above the Ridings just across the North Tyne.

There were other goshawks in the wood, and the original residents were not at all concerned yet, though surely they must have seen the prospecting pair? I went up in the gathering gloom and the beginnings of slow snow to the Richardsons' spring, and lay in the bushes under the new gosses until they had fully settled, in case my crossing their sightlines to go into the house should disturb them. They settled, and in the morning before they were awake I collected a pellet, showing one of them had been feeding on woodpigeon, and the little sprig of ivy the male bird had dropped. They were wrapped in on themselves tightly. The snow had been light, but clung to boles and branches, needles and contorted leaves very faithfully when the wind which brought the snow had dropped.

* * *

coarse-gorse of the gos' eye when it comes at you gold
you lose all-over sense of the body, lose all hold
of the bird, nothing can then be seen or be heard
though the wings shiver, row, quiver, glide
and the tail rises, fans, shows side after side
and the little birds besides are all alarms
and the trees are rivers from her power

eye holds sights lost in the haste, recovered
some passage to the older gods are rendered
sounds that were mixed and gone now one by one
but the bird has passed on now, left just that stun

* * *

Stake Out

casting-collecting

…his already locked-on, undercarriage full-stretch
our legs stiffen on window-blundering following, itch
midges, litchens hail thunder-moments off hawk-perch.
"Hawk parked in Larch" and notebook closes, watcher dozes
on girls half-recollected those fluted out-of-season roses
so never out of season, easily-missed. Lute creaks, hawk mutes
birchbrooms recollected, half-recollected other woods other hawks
other faces, which half-recollected? Shake, hawk up sputum
Keep Awake, Birchbroom's a parasite, composite, complicated
defence to irritation. Hawk bunches carpals, hunches again
stench of his casting that has taken ages of pulses and strain
I take up his menu, again, check, the girl on my arm has bated.
Waiting over, hunger is for tobacco and whisky to follow
what the girl has recollected is that line from Richard Hugo…

Alaska 1973

* * *

This bird, 'West 11', had eaten at least four ounces
of hare breastmeat this morning, cleaned her pounces
and sat around in Newcastleton Forest for ages
whilst we watched a ride's growing redwing assemblages
as she did all day, all the short day so nearby
we thought she must be watching us motionless
until a shedding of redwings, made bold by berries
over-ripe and abundant, in a 'passel' let fly
their taunts and curses at her. 'None of her business'
she ignored them until, in a few seconds of flurries
she takes off, seizes one: ride as empty as the sky…

for Jeremy H.

* * *

red squirrel running drystone dyke top cowers
(the sky is empty of all but a distant caw)
—he has crossed the road between pylon-towers
directly, where I've never seen him before
as if using for guidance, under the hum
of the grid in this summer humidity
and so to the next plantation he has come
by wires that have, unearthed, killed already
today, but what is another pheasant worth
and the goshawk has seen all; his appetite
scorns carrion, swoops on the mite in his might.

* * *

gaining height over everyone
raven speaks to goshawk in that tone
of croak, otherwise as to heron,
taken as challenge or as warning
otherwise-empty sky this morning
and nothing I can see on the ground
—I'm out-of sight, almost out of sound
overnight bivouac under stones
already laid as a dyke that one
of a pair of curlews perches on
fellow-witness of this air-show's fun…

*

their grammars will one day be giving
some other student a new living
developing theory, portent,
contesting a cognitive content
if our hill ravens have held the fells
against game industry's greed that sells
the hills to prejudiced disturbance…

2015

* * *

Gos because

At last into sight
clasps branch hard as bark
opposed scimitars
settle her weight light;
heaviest of stars
mightiest of hawks
sits into starlight

Axehead pierces
entire forest.
Not her prey species,
Kielder knows her best,
assumes the tourist
ignorant. At rest
clasps branch tight as bark
—reflex as killing
severing all sense

Why sit up all night
watching from distance?
Because she is near.
Above, bats replace
swifts for the midges,
approach, and sheer
away canny because
day she soars ridges
they play over, sleep
on the wing she reaps
her forest harvest.

* * *

We were lucky at marten in the woods of Ingleby
Jeff and Stuart and I. We wondered about "good fortune"
as we wandered that whole North Escarpment at liberty
and by 1970, there, and in one daleside soon,
had seen goshawks hunting 'stoggies'; here rabbits had been scarce;
and grouse on the hill—a pair of gosses together, linking,
At Scarth Nick wind lifted dew off fogg grass and heather
once to obscure the great bird's technique; she lost face…
passes at a hare whose jinking lost her… By thinking?

* * *

Writing about what is about; a tautology;
only a fraction of what we are given to see
and that only a fragment of what there is to see
and it is not surprising if our human weakness
runs to admiration, of success, victories of excess
and so we excuse ourselves of, this time, a Crested Tit
—a much rarer bird—not even noticed in the excitement
of a young goshawk; an older one would have been hidden
not so high in a pine that we might have missed it…
But we learned nothing from it, not even the plumage
as it was gone, and the Crested Tit, with self-respect damage…

The Caledonian Forest 1970, with Tony W.

* * *

                              First flight
a function of light wing-loading, well from the start,
turns, banks, pitches, rolls, yaws and even stalls
show the margin-of-error given to each developed part
of the flying-machine in her downy-debris falls
a hundred yards at first, the landing the clumsiest
despite the competent glide, four-foot span outstretched
bouncing on under-carriage. Just a few panic-calls…

* * *

A mind of her own, like any forest fire
to stare a country down
across the northern continents' swollen forests
her wings extend grey-brown
in youth, her eyes spark tips of red hot wire
incandescent to jump contacts
to life from dull textbooks' brittle manifests

               *

Resin crackles and boils in her tight veins
she is direct on her prey
hidden ambush and surprise, not soaring
she watches close, her hodden grey
(even sodden; in these Northwest Coast rains)
attacks so sudden; success
is not her subtleties, but in scoring?

Washington State 1973

* * *

Better than by 'The Hunt'   (my daughters smell death)

Motor of vertical rotors act on suddenly unbound
quarrelling with the air brushed through, marvelling
how this swift soft propeller penetrates wood
we follow ducking, weaving, stumbling forward;
comes hard up against something with a dull thud
a crashing of falling through branches downward:
reaching the ground on a quite different sound.

The hawk has carried away whatever prey already
we find woodpigeon feathers fresh, some ruddled
as if of shepherd's or autumn's pigment, as if leaves
amongst needles, and blood scent spilt on resin's
no other statement but silence breathing in sheaves
of Sitka spruce, Scots pine. Darkness—befuddled
two infants scratched by bark and brambles, blooded.

North Riding 1972

* * *

            gentilis; 'of their own kind'
and nothing gentle about any of it
except in attention at the nest
the pair of demon-lovers must fit
if they are to be 'The Fittest'

if there *are* species, we don't know how many
even of these hunters, 'top of the evolution'—
as recent as yesterday geologically

* * *

A shrill Goshawk's, or possibly a Cooper's Hawk's
so resembled part of a call-to-war song
and ending it, reported clearly of 'Omahaws'
early in the nineteenth century: But were they wrong,
those anthropologists, with their "imitation"
of presumed calls of 'Thunderbirds', a mythic being
when The People themselves' keen attribution
and they say, a 'perfect representation'
is of their 'Bird-Hawk' they are still 'winter-seeing'.

* * *

'Eminence grise' wields power behind-the-scenes
with or without others' knowledge of the means
and this one is out of sight, mostly unseen
by the companies of her potential prey
where they feed or pass by, foregather or play

*

The loners are the watchers, after all
taking-in every movement, every call
there's but one goshawk to forest miles this fall
and I'm not going far from this one today
whilst I stay un-noticed, come what may…

* * *

Tommy and I toddled east from Mickle
"boddened", he said, like "a mule and a donkey"!
heather-burning back of Cronkley
unusual enough for mid-November
before last-evening's crag-streaming blur
of downpours darkening of steaming lava
midnight moon hardly warmed the embers
white hot reddening-round, noon's billows
giving both of us our life-long best odour
stinging the eyes, this bonning the lings
has set nostrils blaring like springs
do. A pair of old war-horses respond
pack horses throw off their panniers
laugh like March or April's strong showers

* * *

For the sun came up only in his big eye
—one eye facing my unwavering long lie.
He had not seemed so close to me in the dark
in the progress of the moon and stars so stark
the aurora couldn't soften though it showed
glancing beauties off his plumage and shadowed
him on to my form from the north. I 'stood by'—
fearing he would fly immediately—
but he was asleep, and I was going to be…

* * *

Followed-up from her stake-out a woodpigeon
across forest—recalling transept—she missed
in a restricted space but for me as grey as her grace
as light-shafted as between spread of her primaries

*

No-one about in the frost of an autumn dawn
I was not to witness any success for her
though she tried close passes of a hazel thicket
since my youth red—then grey-squirrel—haunt
and a roost of dunnocks now. But nothing flew
though much must have caught her eye....

*

I, bent, baffled, bedazzled, by hazel dapples
(kindred on this wind to the shifting shadows
she knows to use hunting the rabbit-meadows)
scents coalesce   wet grass   October apples

*

where she stands tall in dry keck stalks, as faded
her greynesses graded, those fine lines merged
(too many adjectives, this one, to be well versed!)
hawkwatcher otherwise awkwardly just jaded.

Barnie and Easby Abbey, 2007.   for M.H., absent

* * *

                              Gos

at the enormous nest, a stinking four-foot unmade bed
—four eggs incongruous amongst debris of the dead—
the death-deliverer suddenly dropped down from above
as she scooped at my head and removed cleanly
—my woolly cap, shrieking, and muting meanly
down my face, thus disgusting my first, boyhood beard
and I very nearly fell down—as I had feared
since I'd started to climb, startled that big grey wood dove
as if *it* had been a hawk I had been as frightened
—its own nest below I had also hastily so lightened…

              Norway 1955

* * *

Daws over—the pine-tops caw
forming their fear, and for
hawk riding their big-toothed saw
threatens each black-lined life's stem;
a bird of prey, gos tried again,
brutal yet elusive, phlegm
dawn out of darkness, these pines'
harshness, gentle jackdaws' eyes
(emerald, pale emerald)
visible only to them
cold as water inside mines…
Sculpted knotwork through pine crowns
sable interlace lost hawk:
Easily—in sunlight, browns
deceiving as their soft talk!

* * *

ONE

No more than quiver of a forward digit
as I've seen toads express, stalking prey
flicks up an old dry pine cone as at 'tip-cat'
plucks out of air, quick bill, as instinctively

Tosses-up five feet high and as if in play
or for the raquet of   wing to sweep across
send shuttlecocking. I anthropomorphise, they'll say
but Speculation over Observation is loss…

This: one of the entertainments of those hours
watching each other long, he from his tower
me from my bower below, a little distance,
has had some of the scientists soon looking askance!

TWO

Said the Instructor: "now stick to me like glue".
A poem, like any specimen, has its 'presence'
if it is bred-through, its genes expressed still true
a poet can speak of selective breeding, essence…

* * *

so in my ruses I followed the fresh trail-bruises
of a bear along the rolling top edge of the timber
and onto another showing of track; the tumble
of rockfall over old snowslides strewing the finished
old slickenslides where paws and claws had long burnished
the country rock. Shrubby bushes along the jumble
had not come down the chute for a while and this long mile
of berry-bearing bearberry had not detained this bear.
Rim of its ridge above us, cone of its talus below,
we both now wandered up to the lip where he *had* paused
at scenting and to test the air on the updraught it had caused
and still the wind favoured me, and him slowing in the snow
as he left the escarpment to cross the summit plateau.
Only he could know, where the wind was from already,
the far side descended a coulee where he would rest in the sun
roll like a cat with legs in the air making me laugh (quiet, steady…)
and then fall—into juniper-berries I couldn't shun
either, Ruth, fruit he had first choice of, to be fair…!

* * *

gyr versus goshawk

They met on a wet West Cheviot high moss
if only once that winter splintering light
because they expected grouse, and so they'd soar
because spring at last, a rising glow after a night
(if only to them) who can see as far as Thor
even through the roke. And they have come for us
no good to invoke an immortal or Horus
(more falcon than hawk, because much more noble)
their power of (the familiar of) death is also for
themselves and all their own kind, clansmen for war
against themselves, their clans, all that's proper loss.

They have come for us, these the so different
who you think are the same big grey birds of prey
their eyes in the sun, eyes in/out of the sun
(not the same colour at any time of day)
discern we know not but direct each other, shun
each other. Not much more will be apparent
as they shear away on recognition;
(let's say, as Sim Elliott and Hobie Noble—)
this day the grouse there know they can forage on
cautiously until after one has come out of the sun
and the other is gone. The only death that is offered.

"Now Hobie he was an Englishman
And born intil Bewcastledale
But his misdeeds they were see great,
They banished him to Liddisdale"
That gyr hunted both sides of the Border here
considering, working and cropping so indifferent
but like Hobie, so more in trust than fear
more kenspeckle than wily local old goshawk—
he got shot dead on Foulbogshiel, Noble's fatal moss.

* * *

Pained wailing of a bairn, heard again
plaintive, demanding, straight to the breast;
she has ignored red grouse on the nest
for hovering over this hare's form,
raised gentle vortices at her wide wings' tips:
malkin hare gone, the warmth forsaken.
Bent over the leveret, her bill rips
other than moscreepers', latest life of this acre.
She has worked haughlands and flood plains
this spring (until prey depressed by this storm)
for nothing until the wide farms of the Mains.

Triermain, 1986

* * *

March storms, "all-seasons'," clear but threaten soon-returns; and early-arrival redshank repeats sharp alarm-calls echoing round the fellsides—there's hardly a curlew yet—Now blizzards of very fine snow this morning from before first light shocked the pines; a strong wind shaking them so no accumulation on them occurred beyond nooks' and crevices' pockets. Rocks underfoot became unfamiliar, looming larger as the gloom receded into the gills and lightened, at first nearly imperceptibly. The place used by generations of martens on these fells for denning has now been disturbed by the noise and intrusion of keepers cutting a new 'road' for their client-carrying vehicles and their own routine, and seeming unduly-regular quad bike and other a.t.v. activities.

At home, my hazel catkins iced-up where yesterday's bees probed them, leaf-buds barely opening yet some finches attempted to force them open, as greenfinches can. But these were only siskins and goldfinches, and the little anxious assembly was dispersed on the arrival of a slim red squirrel; one carrying a scar across the shoulders I've had the chance to examine and consider the work of a big bird of prey's 'pounce' (in both senses of that word—more likely a goshawk than a buzzard…)

* * *

'Fox and Hounds' crack about the gowk (cuckoo)

noticed that when hawks were "bad"
(he meant numbers were, not habits)
those same years were "bad for gowks"
we inspected the case above the bar:
Cuckoo, and Green and Golden Plover
and the moorcock—the Red Grouse.
"Aye", he said, and that is why hawks
("ye ken, it's the same skins they" inhabit)
arc scarce gowks turn into hawks
for winter, at any rate *by* then
"and, come spring turn back agen"

No wonder they thought them related
closely to each other, some locals
droughty of e'en (none needing bifocals)
barred cuckoos and barred sparrowhawks
"both bothered the poor wee moss-creepers
the one to rear their young and the other
to hunt them down all through winter. *
The barred-breasted, gawk-winged Spar:
I was pointing out when one voice in the bar
had cuckoo "change over" into stane-hawks
shape-shifters, "comin' doon off ft' fells.

"some sparrowhawks will hunt meadow-pipits at any season, of course; but this man couldn't distinguish merlin from spars and talking to others I was clear that they knew the merlin as a winter hunter on the fells 'as much as' a summer one there; the birds often known as 'stanehawks'"

* * *

sixty-five of a hundred landings in trees
in the open or at the edges of woods
were in bare trees, bare branches, perhaps for ease
of alighting and taking off more freely
and surely also   visibility
in fair weather or foul, as if a hawk could
bear getting wet or blown for the advantage
vantage points give at the risk of their plumage
needing more maintenance; do the birds balance
demands of energy and efficiency—
is their 'ecology' their 'economy'?

* * *

Powering deep sweeping wings do not break them
though their nodes seem brittle, sheathes greaves friable;
flowering past, wintering grasses indomitable
yet they register her low passage, waving momentum.

*

She turns aside at the intak's boundary;
old concrete sleeper on end for a dyke post
stretching her wide claws' clasp securely
echeloned wings raised, an elegant bold boast:
our four-ten in range carried for grey squirrels
and brown rats, discouraging cats. No quarrels
with this rabbit-catcher, raised from infirmity…

For the Ridleys (Alston Moor 2011)
(a squab saved from forestry)

* * *

Mistaken for buzzard at the Wall loughs
once with Ken's wintering beasts and neats…
In a minute overhead, when Basil coughed
at Noppins Farm, where the best neeps
were to be had, free for Burns' Neets
at home with him, and at the *Cheviot*
shifting gulls sculling the Ridings haughs.

* * *

Forest Edge, at Anderons' 1956

Bubbling the croonings of blackcock lekking freely
'hopes' of upper-slopes of these hills project them
far downwind, the downdraft of these westerlies…
—though they are alert, ears of goshawks are hidden
and, as in the Border forests for my grandfather
there is nothing but the forester to bother them *
They burble on… something of the cuckoo, the *cuculus*
the singular amongst the hubbub—"all testosterone"
their moving blurs; distance with the growing
drone of many waking bumblebees raising
the ground itself more than chorus; carpet glowing.

* *Forestry Commission policy then was to kill Black Cocks, 'Blackgame' (for damaging the conifers).*

* * *

Trivial, appears prospecting's travail
under idle glory how can it avail
obvious hunter, oblivious of paint
over his own plumage greens and reds rummage?
A show nonchalant in dumb magnificence.
Wavering intention, as ionosphere's,
are the dim lemmings waiting upon his feint?

*

Siege not relieved by her clearing with dawn,
Aurora expands cheering. One rears
on haunches, forepaws relax onto soft paunch;
low gos, pouched in pounces. No time for fear.

* * *

Goshawk hunting under Aurora Borealis, Alaska 1973

The bird hung-about as a cloud; silent, far-ranging,
over only high ground, so stonily engaging
packs of 'fly' grouse, individual hares' attention…
we few, who felt honoured men, I can only mention
those I knew and questioned; one a head-gamekeeper who
compared her closely to all other raptors he knew;
a sheep-farmer, a fell-walker who had "always" wished
he'd not seen her on his own: "who would believe him"?

*

So a hole her size was torn and she fell through unseen
into the view of few, but warned by many corvids between
the Vale of Eden's depths and Alston Moor's eastward spread—
jackdaws, crows, rooks, ravens passing the news ahead,
other birds taking notice a little. Few of men
can read these runes, so no news of nature, again!

Note: *pounces are talons.*

* * *

[from an incident at the Dun Kirk field at Humshaugh by North Tyne, summer 1988 Margaret—one of my rare appearances there and undistinguished save for this incident...]

goshawk that from an apparent indolence
of flight, neglected power in abundance
seeming indifference as that buzzard's soar—
everyday-familiar, yet before
we turn our eyes away suddenly, pulls
on impatience that has twenty drifting gulls
over the whole arc of the sky scattering
urgently; a storm's prelude of spattering
hail driving players in off the playing field
at cricket. I've watched this hawk from the wicket
turn eyes and minds from thinking 'local League Shield'
to an admiration as for peregrines
overhead—the full-tilt chase of woodpigeon,
cleanly struck down dead at the Entrance snicket!

    *

all other-sport forgotten for the moment
by a few there, assuming the falconer
to appear, retrieve the beheaded bird;
no-one came forward, or he let the event
work on the minds of more than this one watcher:
perhaps the same alchemy—it's not absurd—
as changed the mood of the hawk. Who know *what* stirred?

1988

* * *

'Mountain-goats' seem whitesheep to these slopes
tethered—we'd say 'heafed' at home, as if by ropes
watching them forage careful circles, a wonder
at the steepness, still grazing tundra
under a goshawk's slow spiral overhead
far from forest, though its haze has spread—
maybe by the thermal... air thought dead...

Noisy over wader calls had, a surprise,
a peregrine screams intermittently
—and perhaps at the goshawk, perhaps at me
—I can never be out of sight; each watching
all watching. A sentinel wader's cries
disembodied somewhere. My glass betrays me;
but how could a goshawk retire discreetly?

Alaska, 1973

* * *

Woods quietening for the evening; I'd thought of quitting...
sixteen siskins singing their sizzles in sitkas sitting
suddenly stopped sibilants and scolded, squirrel-spitting
here where there are no squirrels I've ever recorded;
wrens, robins chattered, and woodpigeons exploded, scattered
in numbers I hadn't expected. The hawk they respected
had arrived; a goshawk cryptic roost was what mattered...

* * *

'Indigestible' Incident

goshawk caught gowk because gowk
was bowking cropfull of irritance
the hairy pelts of caterpillars
of the Fox or Eggar moths
now at full term and spinning up their
even bristlier cocoons this gowk
had also been collecting from ling
bushes all over the fell
a greedy gowk no inheritance
but my probing of her corpse—
the goshawk had discarded the gowk…

[gowk: local and Scots name for cuckoo; bowk: to choke or retch]
Kielderhead Fell, April 1988

* * *

"There is nothing as perfect as these two crosses and of a comparative date" (they are at Ruthwell and Bewcastle, late seventh-century) "in the whole of Europe" (Nikolaus Pevsner)

Goshawk lifting a new-born lamb, soil and all,
before the ewe could even lick off the caul
—the second time I've seen this. The great hawks came
thirty years ago, advanced, avoiding 'fame'
by elusiveness, or maybe not survived.
To many yet, such great birds have not 'arrived'…

* * *

Bright red cock crossbill this sunlit morning sits
in deep green needles; a child's painted pine cone
thrown up into the branches; they are not yet quite still.
Brick-red cock crossbill as something 'comes over' the sun
a moment that great circle's light meets the will
expressed as the gyre ascending alone
slow enough and solid enough just to fill
the eye of the sun, the other lens once stone
then sand; by glacier's then glassmaker's skill.
Only at this moment I've remotely known
the (gos)hawk's presence above, his opening bill
toward me; then the turning away and he's flown
and the sun warms my face; its relative (thin) chill
calms the pulse, ignites crossbills, a day has grown.

* * *

A poacher and I watched her repel a crow
—launched raucously behind, shaking shocks of black
haunches, ebony polished pounces blue glow
iridescent shoal, hoarse shovelled coal's coarse 'slack'
Dazzling early-air angled light she's rising
though slowed by the wind rocking treetop level;
a clamour of daws, but the crow is prising
some carrion sliver off ryegrass bevel.

Bewcastle Onset 1993

* * *

Boyhood practising for, on sparrowhawks
learning the cadences of all their wing-beats
adjusting to winds and any other burden
—hawks of Rokeby, Wass, Stingamires, Easby;
their kestrels I already knew; came easy.

*

You do not use book study to learn the gos
except for some hints from the best old-timers.
Minds of their own for survival, they were rare
and intelligent to avoid. To know *where*
and *when*; leaving the *why* to grace later years.

* * *

All-seeing eyes in these high Scots pines
I cannot look into the crowns of for the sun's climb
this rare bright April morning arising there behind
where I *think* the hawk is watching me; I'm briefly blind
and this is when he subtly moves; but I can tell where
by the birds between and before us which *I've* never disturbed
which greeted the break of morning grey, but hardly heard
because they were aware of the great grey hawk's presence
—now what is 'sense' which the limits of this 'intelligence'?

* * *

"The forest is impenetrable because there's nothing there"
—to many 'true', but this is only a *non-sequitur*;
ask any hunters, naturalists, 'fungus-foragers'
finding much in hated 'serried ranks' of them conifers"…
Myriads of raindrop, dewdrop, jewels sparkle and shine
fresh leaves—spring-light; this morning's first path through the wood is mine.
The young ravens have flown and the high pines hear singing
drowned out before by raucousness, bickering; the ringing
calls of the birds now are no longer all familiar;
species once lost, and some new arrivals grace the fauna:
spectacularly the nightjar, churring, and the goshawk
mostly silent, and silencing dove coos and pheasant-squawk…
Other recent discoveries I've made, like the firecrest,
rosefinch, forms of crossbills, martens, red squirrels and the rest
foreseen as 'possible' long ago coming into their own
with some unexpected plants, now the seed has been sown?

* * *

A goshawk and a scatter of gulls
struggling in air under a blue sky
of apparent innocence, defined
an Alaskan inlet's true nature
scope for the hawk's challenge, ill-accord
as along many Norway Fjords
winds aloft generate 'williwaws'
(fierce downslope local wind currents
jostling even ravens, crows and daws;
as violent as the Hellum storms
of the Cross Fell range of the Pennines)

* * *

to a murmur of little stirring goshawk passes

Wind lifts beech leaves progressively in a pattern of little waves
a tide towards the wood's enclosing slopes, heaping-up this November
Alan and I looked vainly for woodcocks through. Under the timber
wings blow a path parting the same leaves in lesser musical staves
even the wings of bramblings. A place we had watched a sparrowhawk
gaze and await opportunity, half-hidden in ivy drape
and not stir although we were near. So different this goshawk
for whom the spar shot away, perhaps indeed a timely escape.

to a chorus of wide horizons goshawk soars

Lifting curtains of the greys ascending grey hawk up
wind hacking ragged edges dripping rain sheets
divides curtains for him; for he follows breathing light
whether we call it coincidence avoids the bright
at roost. This his display in March, day after each day
of it he turns over the same tumbled forest side
a focus time determines on an untrodden ride
where roe go early and late, unaware of his mate
of, if aware, I can't tell from their nonchalant gait.

(Border Forests, 1987)

* * *

revisiting boyhood To The Lakes
camping, lamping 'for our future sakes'
with bully-beef in the billycan
live legends of Dalton Millican.

But now new birds are seen, new songs are heard,
there goes that idiot Collared Dove*,
the sort of prey all hawks must love
not too big even for the 'musket'—
(the little cock-sparrowhawk) and yet
for this cock goshawk a decent breakfast
though to most of us he has not yet occurred.

[*breeding since 1962 in the N.W., by my diaries]
Borrowdale (of Derwentwater) 1990

* * *

Co-operation in 'nature' so dramatically at sight:
this hawk's not so different from some clay-pigeon fun;
"scelping" left and right in their floppy taking-off flight
too close together, and saving the use of a scatter-gun
helping us discourage a plenty, penalty, of magpies
today four down in a few seconds and he disdains
to carry any off (distasteful, unlike rooks?) but flies
perches out of our sight, but perhaps watches the stains
spread as a few crows and daws come to scavenge the slain.

Ealingham Rigg and Farm: Walton's.

* * *

Mary come, she'd have been at least attentive
as dumb there she stands for portraiture:
any young woman can look as attractive
if she is as careless and my discomforture
is not her's. My mother attended catwalks.
Thistles ageing stalks as ragged as the hawks',
are the weather's work; she, higher sculpture.

*

Reared near here yet so rarely seen
she stands the riverbanks not as a heron.
Cecil, mending, wall, led by what can this mean,
"too big for a sparrowhawk, must be foreign?"
Sandmartins, then a sandpiper, distracted,
are the other strangers she has attracted...
She lifts, idly as a buzzard and is gone.

(The Wisens, 2009)

* * *

Sept 1st 2000

A great, owl-like in larch branches, female goshawk has been watching me the last three quarters of an hour, after she has hunted very intensely the forty minutes needed for hunting success and on the glade floor, already autumnal (heavy dew, then yellowing grass heads and leaves, that 'scent' of [?burnt something; you may remember from skinned animals?] of opened rabbit. I am not used to a raptor 'sitting over' its meal like this so long with no return to it—they usually slip away (even if, as sometimes, they return later). A few pieces of back and upper breast flesh only have been taken, a few strips this bird evidently now digests (and none of the convulsive movements preceding the ejection of a casting). And 'none' of his behaviour affected by me—I'm sure I've been undetected through the hunt and kill and the roost so far. Found the bird yesterday.

* * *

Brightest of mornings of this airmass deceive;
sun seems at strongest but soon hazes over
wind rises dazing frost-twigsets, mazes leaves
fresh green, freshest green, dull, with grasses and clover
pines and spruce darker with beech and sycamore
the gos has been waiting in, I think, suspense
fidgeting at preening slowly dozing, or,
eyes under third membrane, essential absence.
Long in shelter as the blizzard arrives; for
all hawks forecast a storm, avoid being wet
and blown, yet, backshield facing the wind, well met.

* * *

He knows the dip in the flight-path, the wave-length,
differing between the passerine species
he hunts in this the mature state of his strength
so he can time his follow and snatch with ease.
This morning a regularly dipping flight
keeps a bird in the air, yet gives him his seize;
his prey's pattern becomes his play's prize outright.
Thus this bustling mistle-thrush and fat fieldfare's
flight dwells weakest at its momentary dip
—opportunity that the goshawk prefers
languidly close enough behind, above. Rip.

* * *

Goshawk takes Woodcock off the fell

over recent decades unexpected gamebird nests on the open fell
have included several of woodcock in bracken, often successful
and as hard to find as the goshawks' tree nests so well obscured themselves
though more advertised by the birds' exploding ahead of our footfalls
just as in the woods; their colour-patterns as cryptic and as essential;
our days in the despised fern, as for adders, common lizards eventful
whinchats and pipits, even wrens, loud in their mossy spidered beetled halls

not much escapes, deceives the eye, and the ear, I think, of the grey hawk
overhead; or of the little grey brown falcon merlin, always at work
A feint at rabbit swung aside, stoop grasp and talons forward jerk
marks the hidden quarry asphyxiated in seconds. A sixfold score
in twenty odd years on many fellsides for a thousand such hours and more
nor are woodcocks absent there in winter nowadays short
of the hardest weather, bracken or larkheather and the red grouse court.

Tarset 1987
Stainmore 2010, 2013

* * *

Rainfall on the haughland harder and stronger;
November, old-autumn flatters no longer,
on wooded water riverbanks no more the ingredients
yet where goosander family floats there patience
the river provides. On high crowns over hides
from our sight and theirs the goshawk besides
watches until one of the young buff-heads glides

    *

Then the next riffle ruffles that buoyancy
and a swift shadow overtakes the sawbill…
Brian and I have long been stationary
his rod forgotten as excitement instils
marvelling silence at so sudden and clean
a few drops spattering stones. How alders lean
over along, sheltering that closing scene.

    *

A little upstream those goosanders now ride
as silent and as calm though spread rather wide;
we saw no sign of alarms, this occasion
and wondered at the 'spell' as yet unbroken.
At the nest, once a buzzard's, commotion soon:
quietened only at the rising half-moon.
There were several buff-head feathers, wind-strewn.

Upper South Tynedale 2009

* * *

Goshawk Studies

What promotes discipline from discovery
to let what will grow well beyond reveries
—though allowing those their own vicinity?

*

If I watch the scene long enough I will see
because something develops between gos and me
and once it's there we both have the 'memory'
for at least a week without the boundaries.

* * *

Not cormorant, or goosander, though these might
have expectation's edge for the bulk of shadow
from downriver; a rower of air, dark-grey and white
now low over the water. For me a privilege
when every such surprise so sweetly burns
the back of the neck; no matter expectation spurns
instinct and discipline!, There was an osprey here
a day or two a month earlier, spring of the year.
A violated rabbit squealed, and very near…

Tiptoe, by Tweed May 1971
(no reason the place name should be stranger than, say, 'Shaftoe')

* * *

In a spreading air of not being challenged
—felt in Kestrel's caution and not 'imagined',
their parents shepherding three brash young away
as soon as they see his set motionless sway—
surely he recognises successful weariness
after catching two partridges, newly-fledged.
Evening coming-on, early roost by the river
sky clears as if for how well went the day…
When the 'warden of the marshes' in winter
becomes warden of the fell sides in summer
ringing out for miles—"teeyuuu" syllables
was ever any *alarm* call more joyous
signalling with all their sharp wings a-quiver
Gos watches this progress of sound down river
and its provocation of Oystercatcher
familiar frenzied one after another
swelling to ear-curdling, unanimous.
Gos closed his eyes at such childishness.

(Smales)

* * *

                                        Almost architecturally
—a *beauty* is in the sheen off plumage as off leaves
a burnish of no polish; from the fineness of webbed blades
with ordered rustling in shaking-off graminous sheaves
in their tension from goshawk preening, tinted as long light fades.

Mount Hooley, 1993

* * *

Midwinter dawning black—not yet a morning
looming more than overcast, idly yawning.
When the ice storm came with a screech-owl's warning,
(though they are close together for some warming)
killing as keenly as the goshawk's talons
ice grip final from frozen rain-drench fingers.
Scores, hundreds on and under marker pylons,
Border Forest spruces where winter lingers
longer, for all their helter-skelter shelters:
redwings, wrens, redbreasts, lesser redpolls, siskins
finches, fieldfares, blackbirds, song thrushes, mistles…
A goshawk picks-off a few, scarce ravaging
after a tawny-owl's early scavenging.

                *

I am there for overnight; the martens—elves
who also collected bounty off the shelves.

(Cheviots 1989)

* * *

stands taller than all else upon the tundra
man falters, feeling exposed in such open
but the familiar will warm memories sharpen
of the Northern Moors, in temperate Alaska:
white anemones, silverweed, fireweed,
fresh forest strawberries, orange ochre-red cloudberries
twayblades, cranberries, crowberries, blackberries

for Margaret Hartley and Margaret Bradshaw,
Catherine Rob and Brenda Richardson.

* * *

one of those birds which enlarge the largest skies
the territorial display of the males in March
raises the roof of wherever their fancy lies
phasing their increase over forest—the larch
and spruce of Upper North Tynedale, Liddesdale
Redesdale and Coquet, Spadeadam and The 'Waste'
Chaste Bewcastle offers. Over Tweed and Tividale
upper Clyde and, now, the Tynedales and Weardale
and all so modestly gained, in no innocent haste…

* * *

Far louder than he has any right to be
cock wren, from boasting-post to boasting-post
launches and sustains his morning reveille
and maybe this cock goshawk listens most
of all the listeners at this long wood edge
where the pheasants are silenced by cold sleet rain
and there's glass frost in the grass, rush and sedge;
mist closes-in with the morning—yet again,
the hawk, crouched close in a high pine heady crown
seems alive only at the eyes staring down
for the arrival, rabbits, from underground.

2016

* * *

lost the hawk in flight, low in this forest ride
I stumbled fern stooks, molinia, calluna beside,
kecks. She's as brown this age as all bar Mosses
hunched just another tussock. December woodland
less than two feet high: Young plumage wet as leaves
is it that this bird deliberately deceives?
knowing she gives me no scent, this fitful breeze.

(Simonsides, 1991)

* * *

No 'ifs' or 'buts'?
it was amazing to me, and amusing, to see
ringtail and blue hawk, but not bog owl
flying to the lines of gripps and butts
in a choreography to make me want to howl
and having to holler to myself, but silently
obviously they were enjoying themselves
not dividing the pastures by quartering
chorus to each other, *pas de deux*
did they expect carrion, grouse thrown to dogs?

*

Were they mocking the guns, not long gone away,
over where they hadn't been allowed to breed
but hadn't yet been quite shot, yet shot out of;
though their eggs had been trampled, ßtheir need, their seed.
There came another denial to their play—
a great grey hawk, up from a distant forest;
on former harrier ground, 'lost' irony…
Surely their spirit of place, theirs, revived
to mob even a goshawk before giving weigh.

N.W. Northumberland 1994

* * *

Several times thrusts made at a hoverer
a pass in play, bullying away;
these not pressed home. Kestrel or harrier
graceful or tolerant, not predator or prey
on these occasions. One in ten encounters
were from the start surely not play
or 'rivalry' but bodily assaults, however

*

not 'involved', but quickly deterred and diverted
were scores of corvid 'warnings'. Only the raven
regularly offered opposition, often inverted
with the halberd bill and scutellate. Sable
and angry boasting croaks suddenly so offered
that even a goshawk would take a buzzard's discretion
and not all carrion-crows cower subjection!

(seventy-eight goshawk / kestrel encounters
thirty-one goshawk / sparrowhawk
nineteen goshawk / harrier
six goshawk / hobby)
1972–2016 Tynedale and Tyne Gap

* * *

Where herons teetered as on the breeze
time and sky poised, congregating frogs…
Hammering storm-showers will ease,
thunder-drops burst bubbles, spawn clogs
as higher up the fell on the swelling Raised Bogs

*

Reminded of herons at eels; waiting-on
goshawk sits over the old mine-reservoir
only last week children had been skating on.
Now a blackback* gull arrived as annoyer
but for this pest the goshawk proved destroyer…

North Pennines 1989

**The lesser black-back probably, on inspection.
Many of these nest on the high fells.*

* * *

Watchful as the harriers, kestrels, merlins or crows
daws and gulls, shorteared owls wherever they are yet…
nothing much missed over the miles at tangent, below
though peewits, curlews, call, resent, rise to her silhouette.
long-scanning the "nest-eggs" along the dyke-backs—
those scallops, scoops, of not-yet-melted old snow
neckletting pastures, low and high—reluctant to go
palimpsests of weeks of passage; fresh and older tracks
all to be read by us, if we've a mind to it, daily…

*

but she doesn't like to get wet any more than we do
a flying 'machine' needs care and maintenance. We look
to watch her best when she's flying best under the blue.
Yesterday, from amongst daws she struck a laggard rook
at this season the drying 'lonely wind'* is frequent
and welcome, though cold; only a single swallow
haunts the haughs well into April. Her rook represents
warmth through the cold wet day and night hours to follow,
we rejoice with the Border Ballads' "oh waly, waly"!

from the Commanche: the North Wind.

Tarset, 1990

* * *

Tynedale, June 2008

Light since before 4 a.m., Summer Time, I have a vantage point level with much of the canopy of the pine and spruce wood less than a hundred yards away. For months now northwest winds have been recurring here. In the lee of the rougher winds a variety of small birds, flycatching, launch from their slack-air perches. Flying insects gather, willy nilly, in the calmer air behind trees in such weather; and their concentration is also indicated by the numbers of bats hawking amongst them their fluttering paths crossing each other very intricately and at some speed: amazing manoeuvres as they feed on the wing. The birds are one each of spotted and pied flycatchers, a few coal and blue tits, willow warblers, a robin and seven or eight swallows, even now a few of the versatile chaffinches and dunnocks.

Soon after 6 a.m. and at last, it's been a cool start to the morning, that sign of (high) summer the repeated calling of the woodpigeons begins. Soon after it does so, there is a quite heavy kerfuffle in the pines I watch from this window, less than a hundred yards away. I think a pheasant may be tumbling out of roost amongst them, but that happened an hour and more ago. I see twigs and branchlets to an inch and more in diameter still swaying, marking the short progress through them of something bigger or heavier than their squirrels which have not been obvious so far this morning. The woodpigeons have fallen silent; the only constituents of the dawn chorus here still audible to me, window wide open, are a few blackbirds and tits, a more distant chaffinch; typically of this spring here, no warblers. Familiar with the silhouettes of these canopies of spread pines and spruces against the growing sunlight, I notice the novelty at last, an upright form close to the trunk at the great fork of that fine old pine whose magnificent dividing will provide a clear frame for the sun in some minutes; the fork halfway up the tree's height where I have watched acrobatics and tail-assisted squirrel leaps in its vertical frame through their generations seventeen years.

This shape suggests a giant long-eared owl, even to the ear-tufts, too prominent on the top of the head for that species, rare here; and the form is several sizes too big for that owl. The fieldglasses show that the 'ears' are furry pads on stiff furry limbs sticking up from rigor mortis. The goshawk has a young rabbit in her bill, surely the same young black rabbit I noticed dead on the road here last night as I watched bats hawk. It is clear now; the bird, usually so elusive and silent and rarely seen hunting, has a difficulty with the stiff rabbit. Why did she pick up carrion, and why not carry it in her talons—the usual way? Her bill is fast, possibly in the rabbit's ribcage or vertebrae, and she is trying to shake loose in further kerfuffle and shifting about on her perch until she, perhaps fortuitously, beats the corpse against the two-foot bole near her and it falls free to the ground—where I inspect the rabbit hours later and find bill-bites in scapulars and vertebrae. Was she trying to 'kill' the animal a second time? Was she trying to get it into her crop—an Eagle Owl might have managed that, or a Snowy Owl or Eagle. Why lift the rabbit into the trees unless to feed on it? I've not before noticed a goshawk take an interest in carrion, but I have occasionally known them carry 'trophies' around they had no intention of eating—binder-twine, a glove, for example; much as ravens do. It was a *black* rabbit, unusual around here though I've noticed one or two here and at Whitfield this year. 'Old' Alan, speaking to me four days ago, had watched the day before what should surely be this same bird from the trees by the river near his house launch repeatedly at a blackcock but not strike it, out in the open at the lip of a 'swalley'; the game-bird standing its ground as if aware the great hawk was not 'serious'. The gos had ignored several partridge nearby; which soon, with redshanks and a hen pheasant, made themselves scarce.

* * *

Six a.m. and six greylag fly over north westward low and gaining height, calling. They are surely one of the local Tynehead families leaving for the fells for the Solway or who-knows-where? As they pass over the Black Burn a buzzard-sized bird rises over them from the east and it is a goshawk. The geese rise, toward Black Fell, and slipstream, I think for better speed and possibly the protection of closeness; they are surely aware of the hawk. I've never seen a gos-goose-hawk take a goose and wish *I* was flying and could follow to see what happens. The geese are quiet now, and accelerating, seeming lower as they fly the highest fells and disappear in the distance. The hawk follows them, higher, at about the same speed. Soon, as I continue the line, right-of-way, of an old drove road northward I meet Thomas Nattrass, shepherd with 4 dogs, coming toward me. He has not seen the 'chase' from his pick-up but we chat on related matters, deploring the game-interests' land-use trends…

* * *

Gos and Hare

"Yon gurt hawk, he could do me some good";
get rid of this winter's damn' cat-of the-wood
nibbling everything in-sight worsen rabbit.
Used to have a four-ten, but lost the habit
with rheumatism. He flashes back to the wood edge
before even the old dog can be called, fetched,
but I've got some snares somewhere… try that high ledge.

   *

As if the goshawk had heard (*once* seen by him)
I saw it rise over the trees, though not trim;
was told it had once been a falconer's bird
who had all the poultry in the village scared.
Its boldness didn't extend to hunting hares,
but two youths 'from away' poaching at twilight
shot the hawk for trophy, finding it "starved tight".

   *

Old Turpin, there, the old buck hare there
yes, Turpin, the fast-traveller, he's nowhere
but somewhere else, been and gone, bor, been and gone
and left my good Brussels with 'not a sprout on'
yet he's kept the rabbits off them since the spring!
And, back home, I'd heard of such a silly thing
at around East Harlsey, Lingdale, Pickering.

Shotesham-all-Saints, Norfolk 1974

* * *

for Richard Hugo

Mobbing by swallows flocked, ready to migrate
no adjustment after the storm's straight raking
Stopping my day-journey; you indifferent,
waiting in larch too late to stay in the sun
some plumage still wet from the larch's shaking
silence now purring in, nonchalance, to stun
each of us straightening up to attention…

*

A few years later I am working after flood
the stringy woods are streaking from Balderstone
to Grimshaugh by way of Merryfield, Alston,
Ribbleside coverts, Willwife, and Three Mile Wood
an old gos roost in a bottom by Elston
what seems the same unbuttoned hawk sees, traps me
from the only similar aged larch tree.

*

This gos would go along with poet Turnbull
one of my fellows, written and spoken word,
that what matters was keeping *attention* full
or much would be overlooked and underheard
(he complained that my too-much use of rhyme
as this hawk, watching me… remains laconic
sees that neither of us are wasting our time.

Scottish Borders and Allendale 1991, 1995 (with Gael)

* * *

a young hawk gillside gesturing weakly
caught-up in bramble vines entangled briefly
as I once freed a merlin from a thorn tree;
the hawk surely studying how to get free
as another had worked out a rabbit noose
(or luckily pulled the 'correct' wire loose…)
neither panicked in fear as much as me!

* * *

with Eric Mottram

we sat at the harpsichord whilst she played Bach
he wasn't going to tell me of convoy work
up the Norwegian coast, winters icing hard;
"show me the skin of one of your wild goshawks"
—(travesties but)……"so much bigger than I thought"
No, wrong to consider next raven, falcon:
laughing, "scared more than riding your pillion"!

Bessie Surtees' House, 1979

* * *

Hardly a gentle *gentilis* but well mannered, even shy, self-effacing
and so obscurely methodical in fact, *accipiter* accepted as accurate; a snatcher.
Years in a place before detected as a man can be to uninitiated,
how the children hadn't seen a cow or know of what it, to them, represented

*

'Granny' Grimshaw showed me the rings she'd kept, found under the old high trees
she knew harboured in summer some bird of prey she'd neither heard nor seen
in the Dales Wood which had already lost its red squirrels and its rabbits;
"myxiamatosis" came there in 1951 or 2, she thought. But what about the rings?
They were homing-pigeon rings where there were neither sparrowhawks or falcons…

(1995)

* * *

Michael and I watched rooted as a grey wave lifts itself softly, a ghostly shirt,
long arms suddenly, body puffed fungus, a firedraught, wind down the chimney, old soot levitates
a shape flowering in lenses as well as amorphous powder, rifts of old snow; dust and flakes
shaking snow off brushed branches at last revealing in seconds, great grey hawk in state
little storm rocking bushes lowered to crushing grasses long and dead, a rhythm of its own moment.

Widdale, Richmondshire, Winter 2010

* * *

Beat of the heart to the beating wing,
just for a start. To the light in the eyes
the light in the eyes. Ancestors' totems in birds
as in fellow-mammals; allowed, honoured
hallowed related beings everyone has felt
presences and history free of the academy
natural history and not in the abstracted.
In Box Elder Canyon a hawk too far south
even for winter silently opened its mouth.
Another day's migrant along Kittatinny
'out-of-season', winter. Birders disturbed…

The watching may not rise to a height
of comprehension, let alone to *learn*;
it is the moment, the impulse to delight
something lifts in the bloodstream or the air:
thus even forest gloom enlivens there.

> *('poetry', 'verse', is not competition, "tutors"!*
> *it is merely a little common digestion…)*

* * *

the Scots' scrum-half is sniping-ahead, crushes
clay divots scolding leatherjackets
—grey bird into the rabbit-holding rushes
   pivots left and right on foot
(one launches, the other one snatches)

(Home after another Murrayfield)

* * *

Laconic

incense off the pines is for all seasons good
whether it's congealed or running like blood
as his presence; roosting still clear for me to find
or absence but leaving signatures behind—
table-debris of meals roughly prepared
floating or fallen ploats, pellets from gizzards
(these are to be distinguished from the buzzards',
the sparrowhawks', the crows' and even a scared
kestrel I watched regurgitate in panic)

Privacy

missing recoil of the branch he has left, a kick
in the head otherwise, leaves loud protest the trick
for minutes after the goshawk had gone on
into the sun, out of mere human vision
fast into further forest presence not to arrest
again a year or more in that Woodhead spot
until red squirrels scolding returned him, and not
that he'd been away or at any rate not for long
needing all his thousands of acres. I'm wrong
to think I have more than a few clues
and he will have the secret parts of his dues

* * *

arrival of hawk with hailstorm
a check on breathing; fresh, not warm,
but not freezing the senses, awakening
and the hawk arrives *sighing* as if shaking
still alert for hunting not looking for rest
this springing rhythm is that of speech
where speech is specific natural, not academic
but of the unabashed, and each to each
breathing, walking, gurgling at the mother's breast

Ameshaugh 2011

* * *

On the Wall

Carrion Crow (a big one, but not a raven) and goshawk
a dance in the air this grey dawn, found by one squawk
from the crow carrying on the wind to me a quarter-mile
along the escarpment the wall hugs in its own fine style
How it had started, how far away, and where it would end I
couldn't say, but I followed the dogfight from behind a dyke
for over half a mile and when I lost the pair against
the almost columnar grey crags of the Whinsill at Sewing Shield
they were still intermittently, if not quite so hard, at it.

* * *

we wait until light strengthens
you say, then it's "to our onions"
while he stretches, wing 'lengthens',
slight rasping—from pinions

    *

algorithms of movements
we make of his prey species
perhaps he knows elements
of a still higher facies,
of mathematics, or scents
we don't expect him to know—
ignorance was ever so!

    *

see, he has 'time on the ball',
hunting seems leisurely
when he has options, though small
if 'one' is scarce locally.
But we forget the wide stall
and realities of Plenty;
this week a goosander; but
also the 'old fieldvole glut!'

* * *

Singing, a head

grey as overcast, shufflings on frontal wind
as boot-scored screes grained on mountain sides
grey wolf of tundra and taiga's greyness
grey-barred but blood-blotched she bends working her prey
but light plays off her light steelbill-tomahawk
bill hook swinging,the pheasant not yet moribund

                    *

this little grey beck regularly spills its spittle
spume of its vigour. She drools a dribble soon
her eye gleams bigger. Riffles of her mantling a pride
prize gamebirds. Is that low grumble throat or caught
up off the burn, all gently assaulting ears
attendant, but to what ('ancestral') feelings, fears?

* * *

Hidden nests of the successful goshawk

I've not yet known a nest robbed, of this species
in this country. These hawks are still a novelty;
though I've not known that particular sadness
I've known several birds shot in these forests
in thirty-five years at least that number;
'protected species' status notwithstanding
where 'the law' is scarce and given to slumber.

                *

One man had hoarded a score of such trophies
for sale discreetly, very lucratively
at a distance. Known to a few foresters
he was only once bothered by protesters
as far as I knew at the time; or know now
and I met the international egg trade
apparently empty-handed, openly dismayed…

29/9/84

Early-season that already specified 'Spring' in Kent
etcetera; well before the great hawks' high displaying
Hesleyside's beeches stepladders for stockinged feet or bare
leave the ground behind sooner than most others but old oaks
open up best yet not the sense of being in the air
rather than in a tree's world. Get up through the mists and rokes.
Lodgepole pines and some other conifers tall enough share
impermanence of their palaces, seem such flexible piles.
Birds there get used to you once you are settled for a while.

*

Singing through the fog not the throbbing song-thrush but the thrust
throatiness of the cock mistle-thrush, eyes shut in effort
highest twigs wriggling as if there was a breeze in these taut trees.
    On the next tree, and the 'Keeper and I' had anticipated
    I soon discovered the mornings lesson patiently waited,
    awareness half an hour, but sits my totem motionless;
    a love of nothing else will do; emotion may be mine alone
    but I do not imagine the abstraction of any kind of owl
    deep in his or hers wrapping in and easily caught napping
    traces of feeding gore below the statue, a little feather and bone.

Woodhead 1988

Imagine pattern a smooth stretched proddy;
dolphin-clouds pod the high north west;
on no wind aloft a little spinning body
bounces once, twice, cricket-pitch length
Barnes-Wallis's back garden experiments
but the light projectile that was sent
from far away, a missile token of strength
is what the locals call a "black-cap" finch
(a Marsh Tit or Willow Tit, just a four-inch…
caller-out of "pity-you" from the woods)
high goshawk delivered; why to us?)

* * *

Recognition before knowing is obvious
from taxonomic discipline for us
which like a *completed poem* should
and not like a glimpse does not
exist by itself; a thing of bone and blood
flies off without getting shot
yet lives only in a vulnerable silent surround
which is the start of knowing it, identity
each sort has, if not quite each species found
and named, for not every one is an entity
and every experience is
if the poem follows on the 'jizz'
indefinable but allied to the poem—
part of a same structure; xylem, phloem…

* * *

Fell out of the sky, spaced out along
an upper mud-shelf of tidewater
not so much flock as careful scatter
the notes for an ample parsing song
arising from sufficient waders' clamour
(four species) for anyone, and for any one
of their whichever kind to feel strong
in the presence, well-seen or just sensed,
of hunter or hunters somewhere there
only the sentinels seemed at all tensed
for the cries, the warning-feathers' flare

Thus, quavers wavering in descent
as 'chutes at practice parachute drops
strewn by a longshore breeze, on the crops
sandhoppers, mudworms; on the bent
spiders, sheltering insects, craneflies
much else autolycon, everywhere
to liquid subsongs of contentment.
Then, and do we count the delay wise
ghosting low over the landward/edge fence
cover shortens for all a suspense
goshawk snatches at time, nothing else

At the 1980 Oxford University international conference on the goshawk, attended by delegates from the northern hemisphere range of the bird and beyond, the opening paper was given by Colin Simms, B.A., F.L.S., M.B.O.U., etc. It was a lively meeting with sharp controversy between rival academics as well as good-humoured and progressive concern for the bird itself, Colin's priority being aware of the growing threats to the bird and its habitats; not merely as ikon for birders, 'conservationists', falconers, foresters and 'wilderness' adventurers'…!! (A Russian delegate)

Surely, four hours hunting on to rest
to his roost as cunningly as to the nest
slips between trees at speed which deceived the eye;
like the crow flying low, below shoulder-high
      (And do I know he expects the firearm
      from my telescope inspected, suspects harm?)
no less muscle-memory than the field vole's,
or the shrew's; breakneck speed to and from cover
under the eyes above, late for their holes

so also in fallen leaves, weasel dashes
a lightning red ground strike between my young ashes.

* * *

Goshawk Kills Kestrel

Fixed on his thread, his sharp downward concentration,
the hoverer may not have seen the hoverer overhead;
projected image of himself in our imagination.

No shadows show, this Border sun only a hint of a glow
so both birds, darkened, hang on their own updraught energies
and no thermal convection, spring days in Tarset are often so…

Hen Kestrel, a few strokes, beats up wind from bracken to heather
—her beat from our home familiar miles near—regular
when the hawk stoops abruptly to overtake her altogether
faster one foot on her back before their momentum blurs
foreground and background into those firs that had seemed far
where the beating of wings deaths-rattled, suddenly smothered.

Only later we came across her corpse, recognisable
'Big Blondie' we'd called her; an old bird easily followed
on her vole-hunts. She was little mutilated; breast hollowed
perhaps by a scavenger. Surely a demonstration
of that 'territorial imperative' of our times
whish has us trespassing, one long education…

Tarset, Blackburn Common, with Lesley 1991

shockingly and as loud as alarms of the heron
a pair of ravens off their tree nest, their young within
wrapping round intimately, too close-skin, strident
and these parents climb on their tails off the horizon
to challenge a silhouette hardly growing, still distant,
instantly clear to Paul and I as goshawk coming.

All part of the same urge which has the buds to open
into the pull of pollen and nectar, early-spring
reveals, draws hungry birds from blue tits to woodpigeon;
the big hawk descends to below the tree tops—not ignoring
a sparrowhawk, quite openly waiting for trade
(later, a flycatcher obliges, predictable
little flight from his perch, the return never made)
but the gos; gone, had found all the fuss avoidable…

* * *

This took us to 'The Gay Goshawk'.
For Jackie, who was familiar with it, Basil and Colin provided on the notepad:

    Oh well is me, my gay goshawk
    That ye can both speak and flee;
    Ye'll carry a letter to my love,
    Bring back another yan for me.

    Oh well sal ye my true-love ken,
    As soon as you her see;
    For, of a' the flowers in fair Englann
    The fairest flower is she.

    At even at my love's bower-door
    There grows a bowing birk,
    An' set ye doon and sing thereon
    As she gangs to the kirk.

    Oh first he sang a merry song,
    An' then he sang a grave,
    An then he plucked his feathers gray,
    To her the letter gave.

    He bids you write a letter to him;
    He says he's sent you five;
    He can no wait your love langer
    Tho ye're the fairest woman alive!

* * *

Basil declared there were thirty verses or more in the version he knew as a youth and heard in Redesdale since—a long tale of which the above is merely part of the beginning. So many 'ballads', we thought, are infected by 'Kailyard' dilutions over the centuries—what were some of them, the best of them, like? We then all sang (parts of) 'Sir Patrick Spens' before giving up for this night.

I used to come here to think, I used to come here to pray
watch for or listen for the guidances of the day…
For every thousand or so of passing jackdaws or crows
rooks and pigeons and stock doves and other such so-and-sos
there's now between these woods and forests a good grey hawk
nearly always silent dignity, once provoking a heron's squawk;
now this woodland raven's croak, barking I hear today.

Thanks to such critters, as they come booling along
gos insights come flying and fluttering, falling and stuttering
staggering even into my partly-opened 'sight'; a song
privilege and treasure beyond all my poor uttering.

The Border, 2015

* * *

Scattered little feathers; blast in shale;
crow blown-away-black torn paper crêpes:
goshawk—torque force, picked-up by the gale.
Hanging in adhesive trees. Escapes
only in pieces over winter;
other crows and claws had picked-over.

By Irthing 2014

* * *

Warming-Up and Great Extinctions together, as everywhere aware
on this Waste- and Border land I've always returned to for heart-refreshment
as by your "poems of sight, of sound, of intellectuation", "Disorder"
sharp of bill and talon, as Grey Goshawk bells ballad Bonny Border,
where many modest Marsh Tits call along river woods Teviot, Yarrow,
Upper Clyde, Lyne, Tweed and Liddel, before chiffchaffs come to but offer
dulling of modern repetition. MacDiarmid is culling me; his harrow…

i.m., Chris Grieve (the poet 'Hugh MacDiarmid') 1978, 2016

* * *

CS : immature male goshawk; an individual later to become well-known to both BB and CS (to 1989)

Very beautiful barring and vermiculation, brown cast to grey
(hence of kestrel) (he means female kestrel). BB very excited!
Wouldn't sit on stick to be shown the way out but eventually found
it and lifted straight over the (main) house in a flash (on a strong
west wind). Whilst in the vestibule, nervously shat on his head.
A mark of distinction. BB found a new use for the toilet paper he always stored there.
"When the gods send me a goshawk into my vestibule they can't mean me ill". (It
must have either followed a bird in or mistakenly entered it.) Just beyond the
vestibule, "the shithouse door was shut".

Greystead, October 13, 1983

Later: The bird was handled again by CS, BB and MJG (Dec. '83) when it "showed recognition" (his words) of BB. Colour-marked, it was seen between Stannersburn and Bellingham, Burdonside and Dally Castle. Until late 1989 this bird roosted often at Hesleyside, was watched hunting in North Tynedale regularly: Over 200 castings from this bird were examined by CS and indicated that must of this goshawk's prey were small-to-medium passerine birds (including scores of corvids). Full details are in CS's book of upland natural history.

These flatlands, 'fat lands', yet reveal unhealed
spaces recalling prairie or the semi-arid
Great American Desert, unheard of far beyond,
where trees once gloried; not Wold but Wald or Weald
with wartime airfields everywhere still fade to field
and only bumble bees' drone recalls the bomber 'dromes
bold hares wallaby around their open form homes.

And she takes off; hear her propellers' urgent churning
miles from her brood high in a dense dark old fox-covert
distant, a mirage; goshawk a wavering image, air burning
at an ocean's edge from her ledge; beach beige to lovat.
To this farmer she's a "bluddy moor-buzzard down
from yon Tabular Hills". At least not "that white and brown
eagle" (a winter Rough-legged Buzzard, to his deepest frown).

We found the hawk again, on an elm on Ozzy* ridge
where she'd been feeding on a fat French partridge—
"one less for the Syndicate" One more chance for an 'English'?
We left her to laconic cleaning, preening, flourish.

Osbaldwick

* * *

Above waving spreads of Scots pine broadening at their heads
sky sanctified after aurora burnishing spruce
to my eyeline a fine finial appears, protrudes
yet not apart of this forest; its apex and its dreads;
for forest is silent now despite the dawn, chorus stilled.

Climbed to the nest, already aware of something I had killed;
the privacy, the entity; there'd be little darkness
to help heal. But no desertion by these shy hawks, strong-willed.

suddenly knocked in the neck, dropped to the ground on my haunches
milky-white, it looks like blossom, sky below pine branches.

Norway 1955 (2011)

* * *

landing, steel on stone on drystone capping, cutting its moss
adrenalin, flint sparks to tinder, missing a breath, starts
as a fox sets the bramble brakes warmth afire this gos
pinstripes and sharp-dressed at that; vulnerable our hearts.
Kindling inadequate response, sunset failed ignition
fading fast. He is not to roost like this, in the open;
remember a marten at this spot. He's up, and is gone.

(above Greenhaugh, Tarset 1989)

* * *

Goshawks will be seen, along with kites and harriers
as tourist-income and publicity carriers
as commodities as any 'attraction'
for mass consumption regardless, as by television
what *is* the legitimate 'government' for these birds
we claim to be able to exert over unseen, unheard
mainly for the commercial exploitation of the wild

* * *

The "twitchers" are here, they've heard a vague rumour
or positive communication on the internet
that both 'goshawk' and 'Great Grey Shrike', for heaven's good sake
are disporting on Alston Moor, unlikely season,
and dozens line the roads like a demonstration.
Incurious walkers, golfers, commuters pass by
pass them off as "tourists" without wondering why…
between the O.S. map, the satnav and the pub
(but because of the car so many bring their own grub)

2010

* * *

(After a Norwegian pine forest, I find)
The one goshawk of my pity and privileges
to skin and examine* one of your kind
as is only one, and alleged of a kind

of ligaments, of muscles, of reflexes
canals and soft-tissue, of cold springs,
Working-together as in any anatomy…
but here of course particular, your silent talk.
To the lightning lit in the eye of this hawk

Remembering the old-timer naturalist,
hair as grey, as billowed back as your wing
told me how your flight had troubled him
stared, stirred him from falconer to, content, sing.

In twenty years' experience in the bird rooms of museums

* * *

Though gosses' moulting regime is gradual
lest flying skills be threatened with compromise,
abundant energy, drive, part of the renewal
so that the hunting machine stirs hearts and eyes:
gleaming fresh armour of reptile ancestors
new-moulted corselet, habergeon, helm and greaves
fresh as they could be painted or portrayed by sculptors
new plumage; the old cast off, sloughed, or new leaves

* * *

No-one reads the 'old masters', or so to say…
The obvious questions are hardly ever asked today
everyone getting-on for profit as he may
and she can be required-to. You sit and wait;
sharp gladius in a scabbard of feathers
still quiet August, but on autumn's weathers
bring on, noisy or not, MacDiarmid's "blethers".

Silent birds can leave, give, eloquent echoes
of this summer, other summers, as some time slows
the patterns of incidents the notebook now shows.
Why is it about a thousand dark redwings
came to my pines and sallows, their sweet voices
in apparent enthusiasm. Nothing to eat, yet rejoicing?
You wait. I wait. Yet no executioner's noises.

25 August 2016

* * *

Hawk-haunted trees—the "spars" also prefer them—
shading silence gives us no less strong a spell;
presenting, though they are half-hidden by leaf and stem.
Goshawks provoke golden-plovers on the fell
                              suggest a theorem
of movement, spacings-out maintain sentinel
plangent on their little knolls watching, mourning

*

One season* thirty 'gawdies' were lost to gosses
and peregrines were blamed (and did have a few)
whilst scavengers contributed greater losses
and nearly all of these before they flew.

** 1990; seven study areas in The North Pennines
and Cheviots amounting to 210 'territories'*

* * *

At a first nest of eggs, unable to take one.
Had been easy to climb to, but not easy to find!
Eggs prized alongside those of Golden Eagle, Gyrfalcon.
Pines beside a Norway fjord, pines close together to hide.
Who was I to despoil such a thing, junior "ratcher",
pulse raised to the pitch of winging oystercatcher!
(repeats every time I hear them, this riverside!)

(1955) 2006

* * *

There'd been no night

Above the waving spreads of Scots pine broadered heads
protrudes the more stable tip of one spruce stem in the wind
to the same apex in my eyeline, this line of fine pines,
come mistle-thrush, 'spar', kestrel, goshawk, at different times

*

Balanced in the wind, only a five-degree rocking
even with that extra weight and windage there
gosses hunt, hour about dawn the vigil, fine eyesight
old woods like the Caledonian glens still order
"busy making meat for families" along the Norrland Border.

(1955) 2001

* * *

His long elegancies grey-wagtail-shiver
hissing a little higher than the river,
insists between its stones hardly harsher tones
—his 'contact-note' echoes off boulders, or another
—whose presence close-by water-flash deceives.
Impression for remembrance repeating hones
and gloom under alders downriver receives.

(The South Tyne) for Alexandra 2016

* * *

Distant overall tent-of-the-nomad Blencathra—
A raven crosses from here to there in pulses
we can count on easterlies, Vale of Eden thermals—
buzzards laze between. On-one of these eddies rustles
cock goshawk's April occasional territorial

*

Knows some of the hare's paths, Haresceugh to Souterfell;
the lowland hares, and the best trees to watch them carefully,
more careful than the buzzards, every hare's form a shell
fit for a lambing; more sport than rabbit hunters know well
than that old buck rabbit's crouches the open can sully

*

We have never seen him chase or catch or lift one
but don't suppose bones near his nest are from roadkill.
Buzzard or kite might stoop to that. Evidence is never gone
though it seems transitory as this charnel so rained-upon…
and he has had to learn-over each 'given' woodcraft skill

* * *

Disturbance resisted

on a bough close to the axis, like an owl
hard to see even if you find her, the cowl
of branches, as of a chimney's her shelter
defeats my careful persistent upward stare
she sleeps in deepest shade of high pines, alone
birds lower down seem not to know she is there
nothing to provoke her harsh heckling cackling
which can be, this summer, some softer laughing
a taunt sometimes when I've thought her flown.

*

sometimes her eyebrow lining gives her away
flashing in occasional light, as her eye
will, closer-to: in the pine tops' wave and sway
she is always more live, vigilant, than I;
though the bark ages to a light reddishness
darkening red at dawn and sunset, her tones
grade a little, plumage ready to neutralise
her mature greys reflect less than any bones.
A heron found her for me, coarsely "crank"ing
—she shuffled a little, rattling a few cones.

North Pennines 2016

* * *

…rain eased, and the bird shakes shafts and sheaves, to stretch,
takes-off heavy-plumaged, laboured to a crown hill-mist had left;
wake pursuit of small birds invisible before, pestering as huge insects:
trail in the woods, clear as a contrail's track and as loud in stealth
his sound brushing of leaves, breaking of twigs, dead, a kindling wealth.
…low whispers willow, immense pollen sheddings off old birch, new sallow
catching the breath in catkins; spring's burgeoning I must breast and follow;
so shudders the morning whin and gorse full bushes   on its breeze
whose robin always proceeds at my side quietly, proprietorial:
linnets' nests missed, but liberty of discovery at ease—
his neighbour badger-above-ground another witness at this tutorial.

*

…mid-day haze; see the rowans' cream-blossom-plates-to-be
already yellowing, from green through brown, these longest days
accelerate development, unfinished, as all work is provisional…

*

…eyes which gather so much light, as those day-flying owls might
just deny the dark; this goshawk has watched my progress
and I his stealthily, how his eyes move yet steady: as pony's head
missing nothing I did, riding through the Reservations's distress…

The Rosebud, and Brampton Woods

* * *

Sonnets from Siciliads in Sicily,
equally of music and poetry;
and, some say, St. Francis in his Assisi
—if mainly of a religious ecstasy—
Dante developed his from Cavalcanti
and Cavalcanti so encouraged Dante
that Dante used science and philosophy…

* * *

Dante, the language of the people to supplant Latin;
handle the baggage like a Hutton batting:
angling every stroke-response on merit—
dangling the bat not the sign of the artist.
Bunting's only need the *Eloquentia*;
all technique there, for master and follower
music in all uttered—as after Spenser.

*

Thus Wordsworth and Swinburne speaking the North true
of the people for the people to see through
giving tone-leading each syllable value.
The wordhoard hunter reaches maturity;
after his marriage he took up falconry
and, our gay goshawk latent on his wrist
tradition for the avant-garde male artist…

* * *

Hither and yon he flew hither and yon and again
between the wood edge brambles and the bare glade within
as if unable to make up his mind which rabbit;
whilst the 'hunted' were not hunted, seemed just 'families'…
Weather changing into its nine-month 'winter' regime
with the shortening days and dieback of grass and leaves
more of his bird prey, the several kinds could be seen

Young rowan stems moulting, redden; young alder
are shedding; this hawk watches their arches
whilst bending sallow branches, trusts flying-buttresses—
when threading the boles rests his wings boldly;
even a pigeon needs only most of her wing to fly well
so a goshawk has lift to spare, unless carrying
and can take it easily, when hurrying or harrying.

* * *

Against likelihood

…as it's the storm that comes up *against* the breeze
    — as usual,   the preponderant south-westerlies
it's a goshawk which powers off windward trees
into the attack; the hare crouches in false security…
on a human shriek he's seized by the shoulders
both sets of talons; resistance as if a boulder's
the hare so firm in his form, four feet gripping
in reflex and seeming a deadweight. Slipping
a few centimetres, as postmortem showed
after the goshawk had released his load
—dead of shock or asphyxiation we later found
half a mile away, near enough nest-ground;
maybe because our fault, though we were hidden
and there were hares' bones in the gosses' midden.

(Tarset)

* * *

Mistle-thrush some call the storm cock sings
best, often, before the stuttering of Spring.
One on a tree top, both eyes closed in passion,
was snatched away singing—goshawk 'en passant'
leaving this board entirely clear of pieces
this sky the heavier for it. No instruments
other than 'the aeolian unner the firmament'.

we called this lightest-plumaged of the goshawks nearby after
'Pan'; god of shepherding in the aspens, as of the woodlands
and he took mistle thrush after mistle thrush. Surely an old bird;
an immanence often of our fell between Woodhead's older trees
and the Wark Chirdon forest about Paddaburn, old Tom's piece.
Years later, removed to Alston, he'd speak of that 'haunted' place
he worked alone; my visits and foresters' Giggal and Armstrong
He sensed the bird about "as we often say things, and true"
for no reason we know "we never knew before that we knew"

* * *

Red squirrel hurtles from collision
shock to our three systems
as if a shell whistling past
and of its closing explosion

a shake of three heads at once
some animal treads away,
bird that had fled into sight
the target hit in full flight

hawk struggling in bracken
lifts with the stock dove loud
scattering grey powder and feather
and I might be the most shaken

squirrels scolding from perch
dithering there apoplectic—
the gos, back, a backward lurch
almost seares that squirrel

his free foot of spread talons
snags in the bark of that branch
the first time I've seen this event
so close to a second snatch

ten seconds, perhaps, elapsed
seemed like ten minutes, at least

(Woodhead 1988)

pm, 6 Jan 2016 by the river Irthing

Paired jackdaws emerge; some of the cock birds start flying stunts
afternoon drying, lifting after weeks of rain and floods
such times I've often noticed raptors urgent blood-feuds, hunts
and their prey also need to be after foraging food
runs of rabbits and rats, voles and moles despite beaten-down grass
these lines show through from the height he's flying, prospecting, at
resident goshawk, flown five miles, has not yet made a pass…

From his post now a field of dockens becomes troubled
its drying wind though the goshawk hums as through thistles whistles;
I am too near, hide breathing with caution redoubled
but he takes off away, no eye-to-eye, but he bristles
like hawthorn; up rise a flock of goldfinches I'd not seen
he shows no interest in, but against distant trees' screen
pale woodpigeons parade clumsy flutters on spruce green

He is over them and behind, rowing hard, very fast,
somewhere a heron alarms, and jackdaws' cackling chorus
I don't see the snatch, but the heavier goshawk is past
and the present is that bewilderment—not nothing for us
for we have been hunters; and, some of us, slightly aware
or intensely engaged at the fringe of emotion, scare
the goshawk is big enough to deliver, and, so, rare.

* * *

beating low and slow, barely holding weigh
more as a harrier or owl, resistance
into the wind; against summer grasses' dance
wavering about as any cattle—stray
deceiving or intriguing rabbits. A glance
and the goshawk strikes while (just as I'm away).
No noise, no flurry, no shadow-play…

La Rouergue, France (Fabre country)

* * *

Spaced-out over this Marcher March sky, yet rather a few
cock-goshawk's high silent spirals, and not the buzzard's mew
declare the presences; a kestrel also painted like new
—light chestnut brightly burning, the grey looking blue
watching with me, the carrion crows and jackdaws
cruise and patrol. Haven't heard raven's croaking caws
since the goshawk got up, but two were here at dawn…

* * *

Though here and there anemones, foxgloves, bluebells shoot
and some fine fungi push through the spruce needles underfoot
 and the hawk's kills accumulate to stay to be decayed
the forest is to be cleared, 'cropped', its essence dismayed;
deer and most birds exiled, red squirrels banished 'for good'
and its ride's privacies exposed; for fireweed, mat-grass
its fox or marten, spar or goshawk gone-away at last…
but harriers move in for a few seasons, or bog owls
haunt as silently, perhaps nest, listen to moor-fowls
and the voles attack the fresh carpet, attracting many
—the kestrels, barn owls, and the lesser weasel family.

* * *

Statistic I

At their feeding-tables, spendings of remains
—but several species of North American 'hawk'
share and or overlap their hunting domains
                                    goshawk

                   squawk

              black-oystercatcher, mollymawk…

Statistic II

Ball in hand, foot round a round thing he has freed
at some hustled speed, sport of passionate need
flight zigzagging a little: determined though
snow loosened on spruces this sunset they bleed

Past where I stood, for a trail of blood *on* the snow
his kill a thrush. Just such a touch of the flow
I feel the rush go………and his register grow.

* * *

Should it be so expected, so apparent
that each bird of prey is in an argument?
Who can 'prove' plan, evolution or intent?
Darwin's apologists, also 'Darwin's Ghosts'
are out there, shrouded, sitting on their fence posts;
in the tops or laps of trees, on crags, on walls;
yet no-one, so dumb, will learn their calls

* * *

First emergent from the mirk the dark stark pines
the same tall trees of kestrel, buzzard, goshawk
wind rising morning clearing sight and flight lines
a kestrel, tempest-tossed bobbing tawny cork
gusts of force nine embarrassed at Falstone mines
opted for lee-sides of dykes. Overhead Hawk
saw where the buzzard as so often, declines
chance of rabbit in the windy open fields
perhaps has scent of roadkill near The Shields
Goshawk will wait until some vigilance yields…

* * *

Above, only the buds, below dark green seaves.
Silver-and-gold, catkins and new leaves
not to be burnished, soon to tarnish
this short season rattling renewal.
Though he brings her a spray of garnish
or to furnish—at least it cheers my mind
as she arranges it at the wide nest-rim.
Anemone the woods sprinkle and the kind
of decoration Harry tucks into his hat-brim
on his peregrinations—kindling or fuel…

Brood over her chicks' useless flutter;
constant bicker, hungry restlessness,
watchful steel-bill, once their recklessness:
eye as yellow as hill-farm butter.

* * *

his broad wings float in on the morning, low out of the sun
dropping his undercarriage down in this silage-cut aftermath;
playful flourishes, wings, neck, legs, giving me sense of fun
prancing before wallowing dewy grass sparkling to his bath
—only early August, but just smell the damp in the air—
sandpipers, ready to go south the only other birds in sight
no jackdaws, no passerines populate a general scare.
The same bird ten days ago dipped-in at old Cadger's Wath
washed carefully, setting-up a sandpiper's family flight
up to his axillaries, not caring that I was there
and a curious kestrel, before the falcon took fright.
He stepping-stoned (as once before near Hadyard Wath)
jumped up into the wind on a post to spreadeagle bold
as a cormorant in those illuminations of old…

North Tyne haughs, 1988

* * *

Onset in reddening sunset now
its farms gladdening the eye
its buzzard familiar overhead
its kestrel showing a rudding prow
hanging into the westerlies over voles' rushes

weeks ago over its Kye
incomer—Kite met the west and bled
even a 'ringtail' harrier blushes
an hour before the scene stills and hushes.
Distance materialises a goshawk
from nowhere out of a sycamore fork.

Bewcastle '90

Take the day, be it never so grey
before the hawk sets out at hunting
—stay steady and study the situation
grey hound 'Hønsehauk' in the slips, ring
be with him one of those the rain won't soften
and we don't pass this way too often
don't leave a field with this fine array
setting acres of yowes' ears up
as if scenting, not hearing the tup…

He still hesitates, shaking his bow
as the falconer's perch now the bough
now flying, to be almost unseen
sharp thicket to thicket, wicket to wicket
runs the gauntlet of sentinel birds

a gambler on the occasion, of the occasion
wagering grace—no effort wasted
on the outcome—killing no disgrace

grey in the tree crown, then against the blue;
as we find the nests by looking through
against the light, and we start again…

* * *

Blind, we scramble in a nervous selfish rage
after what *they* tell us is our heritage
whilst we deny some ancient/original inhabitants
rights to their (largely unknown) continuance—
sure signs of our ruthless ignorance;
the great grey hawks, nevertheless can advance
though we cannot name the players on the stage

Nation of dogwalkers and drivers-around
within only the accepted sight and sound
of screens, gadgets, constant 'communication'
of the bland and commercial "self expression";
this self-effacing hawk stalks imagination
for very few—or his extermination!
(by commerce, game industry, the blind surround)

* * *

As a 'skipping stone' thrown, skimming her billow wings
gos catches in the shallows, so shadowed by sallows
one grasp of a brood of teal, of little followers
did jarping heron know, set drinking cattle bellowing?

We follow-up to where she tends brood "in their blethers"—
good legs; almost, in a short skirt, but of floating length
she dances, curtseys, at her work of ploating feathers

1988, with Ken Pick

* * *

At Bewcastle Cross, aged about 1440

White shite of "Corbies": Crows or Raven, maybe
when Basil speaks of jackdaws, he says 'Hoodie'.
Running a rabbit from its base, a stoat…
Bewcastle Waste seems engendered of old bones
—in tone, texture, shaggy as its herds of wild goat;
has tumbled for the masons in its Anglian zones
one of its grey-weathered, gritty Fell Sandstones.

Quarried off contorted tors, which seem to float
as if thrown, to exhibiting erosion's notation:
there's a blank awaiting sculptor, cross-shaped hollow
as if for a grave, or where the Cross or its fellow
tooth were extracted whole, extracted in isolation
of a gospel. The Apostle's arm, my calculation
carries a goshawk, witness to lord and Lord

And carries it as staff, guerdon, sceptre, sword
while we watched, over Bueth's Castle there soared
where we'd seen buzzards and kestrels, great grey hawk
back from antiquity, age of ancient raw chivalry
translated or not; the place, the runes, roared

* * *

Only for a moment, regretted being there

Dawn's nor-westerlies, ridden them there by the little Brough
to a sudden stun of their blusters (buffeting enough
for one morning) the storm still in a (minor) gill-brack
loud as clouds had been over my Simonside bivouac
their thunder round and round as if the fell was all sound.

All arms-and-legs swinging, less lordly and more scruff
she comes a-tumble out of above, barred featherstuff
stalling at last-gasp grasp at the starling flock folk
overhead out of nowhere; shocked, I stumble and choke
she's standing and shaking in the bogmoss's waving, quaking.

She gathers her dignity draping striped petticoat
watching aloft the starling cloud reform, and so float
that shape-shifting is re-established and a sky burnished.
Her eyes re-kindle to reddened glowing blast-furnaces
—my being-there surely the excuse for her glare

She's broken my cover, better than from above,
where the black maelstrom makes feints at mobbing
Do these celebrity clubbings express some kind of love?
They hardly drive their demonstrations home. A little feather-robbing…
In minutes pipits rise off the moss. No lost surprise.

(Border Mires, Winter '80/81)

* * *

COO, COO ... COO, COO ... COO, COO

a spirit of the Groves both above and below
with the Crow and his ghost the Hooded Crow,
Ettrick Forest to the plantings on Stain-more
whose blue-grey doves plump-up the store,
their double—single note a re-assurance
insurance for their hunters. Goshawks' stance
overlooked as novelties invariably are…

air-currents enhanced by their displaying
You'd think these goshawks deliberately playing
with the more balletic Stock doves' grace
tumbling and gliding through lower sky space;
of all hunters, even the most 'in-your-face'
are yet the least known, found, recognised
parabolas parameters, tapestries mist-incised.

1991

* * *

Return of the Goshawk

When in storms the arms of sallows and willows
and even stiffer trees are grasping for rough embrace
of the immaterial, threatening the hunter
and no other will fly through but a great grey
intent on capture, careless in confident rapture;
no, not the dashing sparrowhawk or merlin—
then know the goshawk has returned to Britain.

Generations, centuries of banishment;
by arrow, trap, gun and prejudice
denied from nature's ordered place by man
a place at the head of affairs, at the table,
is now returning, unseen by those ignorant
of the forests, of beauty of necessities
as Mercury descended, on an oarage…

On an oarage of wing unexpected
of span and speed and sudden-ness; arrival
and in those forests passed-over as useless
as indeed for mines closing, papermills for the ether
open ground lost to grazing, even agriculture;
figure of the closed-off minds of bureaucracy
'planning', over-ruled, as ever, by Nature!

* * *

Degsastan

Out of this narrow pass between the rivals
a long history, tradition of leavings and arrivals
Scotland and England at it, as ever were
bird of broad wing to prey, from spur to spur
interlocking the narrow road, the Dawston burn
talk of the Ardennes for a surprise
or of the defile of Thermopylae
Once, for John Bulmer, Basil Bunting and I
the only Golden Eagle of along the broad Border
over our heads to soar low down Liddesdale
free of twitchers, of persecution, of being *seen*

* * *

Plenty of rain every day and every night, it seems
and this hawk, as others of the raptorial kind just gleams
in it, 'resting on his laurels' defiant, exposed on his pine
in a solitude daily, nightly, I'd supposed was mine
he must be killing somewhere, or eye and wing would not shine…

* * *

For Nick, former forester

You who love and tell historied forest and space-enchanted hill
I wish you further joys of these with age; for these renew us still!
The Tyne's 'tamed', but yet spirit lives as with a goshawk's kill
unknown outlaw; bold merlin of the rocks another thrill…
MacDiarmid told me, it's a wonder any Border liveliness persists
but we take our pleasures as the rocks are scraped by their mists…

*

In years to come, at this rate, even the curlew will be less present
to fill our air now the cuckoo, 'gowk', becomes almost absent
in the self-defeating progress, 'popular' "recreation"
our land is limited, and won't abide such domination.
Go on printing the legend; words that outlive extermination!

(Nichol Short, born Garrigill; the best dialect verse)

* * *

Goshawk takes new-born lamb

One of twins of a Swaledale yowe
and something I've not seen anywhere before now
Goshawk female, brood-patch showing
from nowhere over my head, I feel the blowing,
made no attempt to choke or tear or slit
no picking at eyes as I've seen 'corbies' at it,
but a short approach on the ground, 'a waddle'
and picking the lamb up sharp by the saddle
carried off the prize, legs trailing, head sagging
to tree top height she, and apparently flagging,
crashed away through crowns, bloodless dragging

(near Sleetbeck)

* * *

Below, a mist of light green bloom glow the thorns
but for spots of old blood where there had been haws
ripped and nipped by frost—thrushes a goshawk
has taken deadly daily a week and more;
Full days for us dully counting through this cull
and at other places, all such losses ignored
by other birds but for their panic and talk
and the mobbing by some frenzied few again
and again. Reduction at their roosts explained.
Goshawk forty per cent success the average gain
at every attempt; only early-morning stalk

* * *

As I was singing

Young hawk in lifting beech leaves, woodland floor
I had not thought to look at first, before
the carpet russet shifted to its new shore
against the rabbit-riddled bank where a score
of them hid underground, would there be more;
would the apprentice react there in front of the store
closed against him? Would he examine any door?

*

Did he know I was seven yards behind him, waiting?
Indifferent, the wind, all morning so aggravating
to our impatience, even in trees above was abating
and the stillness I feel of some hardly-relating
dream came on and, a confidence inflating
as his mother might at feeding him, but not stating
anything I was sure of, of course. He wasn't 'bating'
but spreading forward one leg and each wing
mantling over a prey, a gift of food she'd bring;
he didn't glance back. And a young rabbit was coming
down the bank, willing him quickly killing.

* * *

August is their quietest month
striding woods silent from the first light
dumb all day as if without incident—
humming as if of insects but not quite
to subdue the rustling of foliage.
Nesting over, questing reduced, moult
set-in for most birds, with dulled plumage.

August drowsily relaxing of us
spruce branches drooping under their weight
new growth hiding spread bird families
(gos hunting has done unseen damage)
(sparrowhawks and owls taken their toll)
blown feathers collect in undergrowth
modest witnesses to the carnage

Blackbirds that dashed a look out bows
swearing loudly all those weeks ago
even companion robin of that age
                              the wren?
and I can't find the signs of goshawk
even in the transepts of this stage.

* * *

Goshawks shot

"I use goose-shot", appropriately, 'BB";
I was surprised he opened-up so, to me.
He'd helped keep "a clean forest, most of his life
before the bloody big hawks had arrived"

*

And that means "mekkin sure their lives are shortened"
—he never, like so many, could find nests; "not important"
He last had shot a young one, still a mass of brown
—like other buggers, buzzard and heron "*bring them down*".
Yet I've always had more time for the 'old-timers'
than for experts; politicians, and social-climbers.

1998

* * *

Some too conscious of criticism today to display
their gibbets, 'coats-of-arms', and don't they say
"these silly ramblers nowadays get everywhere…"
this goshawk was half-buried but only half-just-there:
some dog or fox or badger scavenged, "dug up neat"
—and I recovered the remains, melting-away,
of that great true hawk, less the best meat…

2006

* * *

But   an eye-opener.   Eight fieldfares at rowan
squabble over carmine bunches. He flopped down
for once under high trees including his lookout—
one eye on their feeding frenzy, one on me
for minutes those had given the thrushes, time to flee
what was he doing, walking 'drunken' on the ground?

* * *

Dipper dithering, bobbing on his chosen stone
midstream for a snatch of February song
before repeating over the current's drone
intermittent, but all of eight minutes long.
A shadow, and a quiet moment's breath
and empty stone he has not dived from silent.
But downstream a few fresh feathers—breast
the riffles reveal, they ride a wavelet's crest.
Goshawk ploating revealed the rest.

With the leaves off the trees, they go for other cover
they can see far from, discern of their Earth all around
their sky from being unseen; even to my pines whenever
fed and to be preened; their way of just going to ground.
To watch then from being unseen, easy in fine weather
—of course to me mostly unrewarding in times of storm—
like falcons they require to be dry, to hold—together
aerodynamic plumage ready, to keep hot blood warm.
I've been undercover already three hours this morning;
too complacent, and missed her taking-off without warning.

* * *

Goshawk unable to halt the headlong chase
as the stock-dove dropped into its ground cover
landed further in its sprags, entangled there.
This happened in Tarset, where six bottle-tits
reared nearby in a felt-pocket nest
in the dove's home thicket mobbed the intruder
their noise and vigour made up for littleness

a hawk's pride cannot be denied; not this one,
no escaped "falconer's bird". As a great herd
that seemed every birdlike presence for miles
descended crescendo within feet— seconds
but the hunter bursting free swung both talons
widely and wildly scorched off with two or three
leaving a fletch of flight feathers for me

1990

* * *

Boldest, proudest of the True Hawks* race
breast fine chain-mail, no link out of place
collar and corselet overlapping
armour tough against tearing, snapping
sword-sharp claws of steel, greaves of gold-leaf
sinews battle-stretched, often and long…

*The *accipiters*

steepling spruces taper to spread their spacing
as calls separate the feeding birds below;
a pattern moving through. My senses racing
deceive, or have me believe, watching the crow,
that there is more than his kind also tracing
those movements with me, though nothing yet to show
my second-rate awareness what to follow

*

wren silent, then robin, at my elbow go
a furlong relay between then, just pacing,
no warning sent ahead. My progress now slow
as silence; no thickets ahead for facing…
these are the moments I believe that we know
long histories of hunters we are tracing
no matter how small the fraction we can know

*

not today we'll see the grey goshawk gracing
a stouter tree, and so slightly shaking the snow
or elsewhere gliding over the ride "casing
the joint" where the clearings meet sunlit, bestow
visions of serried panicked rabbits chasing
each others' scuts, warning signals all aglow
in the web of place a broken thread, yet lacing…

Kershope Forest with Tommy 1998

* * *

of home

a World within the crown of top-spreading Scots pine
of one Scots pine the most favoured because it is yours
and apart from, yet of, the neighbour I can climb 'mine!',
I cannot enter the inner privacy of. There stores
of your history of I can observe only a fraction
is 'one little room and everywhere' to you
when at home; a night or a day's satisfaction
sustained by prey, and who knows what emotion
gives rest and restless news to me; a little of you.

1991

* * *

there is something in any name deeper than the skin,
in any image there is of the spirit creating in
something strong and needed is there in, there in
for revelation, a moment seeded, not speculation
necessary for any kind of fuller 'education'
because it is a 'leading-out', just an indication
we partly, only, name as "inspiration"—
and of that magic, a feathered warrior, a chief carrier
comes across a little of its sky, granted to us now *gratis*
not the circling cambridge or milky blue of cock hen harrier
Circus cyaneus, but the great grey directness of *Accipiter gentilis*

* * *

At the nest of gone goshawks 14.9.2016

Less nomad's rest than a summer's home
this treetop homesteading's twig-basket
—built by crows or magpies (the dome…)
—the gosses added fresh green, as by bucket;
many wings of bird prey, legs of rabbits,
pellets (and on the floor of the wood, below):
at end of season I make minimal tally
of what some of this charnel can show;
of what abundance in this far valley…

(Woodpigeon 15 plus, Stock Dove 3 plus,
Ring Dove 3 plus, Magpie 2 plus,
Mistle Thrush, Blackbird, Greater Spotted Woodpecker,
Partridge (French), Domestic Hen, Jackdaw,
Mallard, Teal, Redshank, Lapwing,
a young Curlew, Wrens, Water Vole, at least
11 rabbits and 8 rats…)

(Tynedale)

* * *

Teeming rain, and promising to come again
kept this bird of prey in short sheltering larch
bent-over already a mean century
of no great hawks' occasional tenancy
for all the woodlarks answering high skylarks
and windy storm cocks declaring sovereign

*

Each of these, the skylarks taken on the ground
had been tasted on this larch in this late spring.
But woodpigeon legion, at little distance,
fidgeted, not yet fat. He gave them scarce a glance
this morning, and hunched dry in comfort and, warning,
parted a spittle mist in the slips, a hound…

*

Then dropped out of sight, took the brackens' snicket.
Sudden sodden feathers flew; stoggies' thicket.

* * *

from Rhymes of a Country Naturalist

I'd been riding; oh, you know the one—
11-50 Brough-with-the-sidecar-on—
on the sixth of June in nineteen-seventy-one
my job following-up a farmer's complaint.
oh, memory neither weary nor faint!

*

Hill-pasture and hayfields and no frills,
"chickens gone missing" by the Hambledon Hills…
The climb to the nest gave more view than thrills;
partridge and grouse poults; this hawk is no saint:
my diary neither weary nor faint…

*

Not to exaggerate the threat to his hens
but recommending no action to be taken then:
"those fledglings have the law's full protection"
gladly aware, no nearby keepers of game
—'Report' and memory not quite the same!

*

Goshawks I stopped short of advertising
they were rare, but their star at last rising.
Nature, for her devotees, is always surprising
and goshawks somehow getting their own way
at last. Which, in cause of Truth, should we say?

1971

Assembly of hirundines, as to migrate
over and from this coast at Anstruther
busy feeding-flights and display flights
getting-in-the-way of each other—
a young gos and an old kestrel, late
on the scene, according to their lights
patrol, feint, or fuss each other also
and one is not keen on any swallow
but buffets the other hunter mildly
(the kestrel at the great goshawk wildly);
I stand by, *part of it, but idly…*
So very pleased when another knows
a goshawk, what naming them bestows
and then is discreet about it, shows
caution as well as excitement
at beauty, at fitness-for-'purpose'.
If no-one else is taking notice
—the case, for example, dog-walkers—
so much the better. Avoid incitement
to 'twitchers', 'falconers' (as hawkers).
Let every living thing its chance;
rejoice also in the humble presence…

* * *

High-Fells April 2011

The mood-music goes a little ahead of the action
to anticipate, for we have hunter's brain, reaction
this morning the golden-plovers each take up the same strain
of warning; territory after territory, gain
urgency from each other, three-dimensional chain—
or, if you like, just emphasising a people's refrain
of solidarity facing an unknown intrusion.

*

for the alarm is general, they don't yet know quite who
approaches and traverses; though at the head of the queue
the first-responder may have a clue, a code to relay
as to whether fox or dog or crow or a bird-of-prey
a heron or mankind, raven or cat or 'weasel', say
but today I see low over the way for once, grey
the Goshawk, not the grey Bluehawk harrier anyway…

*

and the sentinel cock plovers rise almost together
away from their mates, in unhailing, in moss and heather;
their crying and apparently wild haphazard flying
as the hawk dithers at first, then he's forcefully trying
to climb on his tail; soaring here would be just tying
himself in knots in the confusion and mobbing and crying…
he's away; today none of this community is dying.

* * *

'Essential Elements in the Calculation': The Goshawk Poems of Colin Simms

When Colin Simms read his work for the London reading series SubVoicive in the summer of 1990, the occasion was not only a rare visit to the metropolis but also a rare poetry experience. The poems emerged, quietly spoken, with considerable care and modesty, as powerful records of experience that most of the urban audience knew nothing about—non-urban, and avoiding the current conventions. The voicing of the poems arose from a long career as a naturalist, from a care for hawks, lizards, otters and other wild creatures, and from his own appreciative presence and conservational lifelong accumulation within an essential and difficult ecology. But this is his location for detecting the structures of human and non-human lives. The second section of the present book considers one such metastructure, the wheel of the seasons. These four sections (previously published as 'Goshawk' in *Figs,* but here revised) present syntax and cadences of a particularly spatial length. Human beings are seen in 'winter' poem 1: the detailed peculiarity of Northumberland men working a tractor in their land, war news entering their labour structure of existence. The goshawk is imagined in *its* particularity from observational data, *its* kind of laws, and *its* violations of fellow-life—the squirrel victim. Then the word "laws" appears within the intensely active detail. This is not some static landscape considered from some kind of 'above'. "War" and "hunt", and what the dying in winter necessarily brings, are placed *within* a clear vision, into which the term "confidence" is entered for definition. Colin Simms is working in the finest traditions of writing to cope with such given existentials, but his poetics are his own, challenging customary grammar and sequentiality in order to maintain the accuracy of the life detail and its movements he knows from experience.

Goshawk Lives is masterly in its kinaesthetic language—all senses interactive as they are in our lives, especially when freed from some of the man-made enclosures or the settlement. It is the language for the basis of knowledge, and the usage is happily free from nostalgia, the blight of the wordsworthian. The poetry exhilarates in its invitation to participate in the verbal presentation of so much care for fact, and care for the maintenance of fact. But this care includes meanings for relationships between "protection", "fair game" and "law" as they radiate into everything human life does. The sudden focus on plant-galls and the goshawk young in 'summer' poem 3 is Simms' "news that stays news", a disturbance of the commonplaces of bland sensibility trained to believe that the words "nature" and "natural" are placid and static, and that urban existence is prior value.

This disturbance factor is a sign or the unease of good poetry and its controls as they challenge the common lie that art is for comfort and reassurance. Simms writes away from rooms, shops and lecture halls. The '60s diary note (near the opening of the first section of this book) records a wonder at the goshawk's particular perfection that could only be humanly registered in patience and a slow accumulation of information. The bird's speeds and pauses have been learned by a man who knows how and why to slow the pace of life and yield to the relative stasis of watching and listening, a life alien to the empty accelerations or dominant life-styles in our asocial technological heap.

In some poems in this section Simms needs to make a prosodic design of spaced-out measures in order to slow down the action and habits of poetic linearity. He requires extracts from overtly offered diaries to reinforce the sense of direct record, something in the manner of Kerouac's sketching. One crux is contained in 'Hunters in the Wood', as ambivalent as Thoreau's acceptance of hunting and rifle-training for the young, within knowledge of the natural by contact experience. The densely structured 21-line paragraph includes the poet as observer of both rabbit-shooting and the still watchfulness of the hawk—two kinds of predation. The poem is followed by **a** passage from Chaucer's 1380s *Parlament of Fowles* on the hawk as "tyraunt" with "outrageous ravyne". So these, too, are major parts of what Thoreau called "essential elements in the calculation".

The prose text of the last section, titled from the Northumbrian poet Basil Bunting's birthday, begins with a relic of stone-age hunters being found near the Simms' house near the North Tyne, this being watched by **a** pair of goshawks. The prose is calmly paced, even subdued, and moves to include the larger space of Northumberland, named as well as presented, and also the work of the ornithologist who collects a hawk's pellet to examine its diet. The atmosphere is one of inevitability, and the work ends with that kind of active silence that surrounds and imbues Colin Simms' life and work, the instigating environment of his very special poetry and its articulation of what Thoreau termed "the neccessaries of life".

Eric Mottram

www.ingramcontent.com/pod-product-compliance
Lightning Source LLC
Chambersburg PA
CBHW081133170426
43197CB00017B/2850